THE UNMADE FUTURE

FUTURE

HOW CREATIVITY HAPPENS

ARVIND UPADHYAY

This book is about creativity, based on histories of contemporary people who know about it firsthand. It starts with a description of what creativity is, it reviews the way creative people work and live, and it ends with ideas about how to make your life more like that of the creative exemplars I studied. There are no simple solutions in these pages and a few unfamiliar ideas. The real story of creativity is more difficult and strange than many overly optimistic accounts have claimed. For one thing, as I will try to show, an idea or product that deserves the label "creative" arises from the synergy of many sources and not only from the mind of a single person. It is easier to enhance creativity by changing conditions in the environment than by trying to make people think more creatively. And a genuinely creative accomplishment is almost never the result of a sudden insight, a lightbulb flashing on in the dark, but comes after years of hard work. Creativity is a central source of meaning in our lives for several reasons. Here I want to mention only the two main ones. First, most of the things that are interesting, important, and human are the results of creativity. We share 98 percent of our genetic makeup with chimpanzees. What makes us different—our language, values, artistic expression, scientific understanding, and technology—is the result of individual ingenuity that was recognized, rewarded, and transmitted through learning. Without creativity, it would be difficult indeed to distinguish humans from apes. The second reason creativity is so fascinating is that when we are involved in it, we feel that we are living more fully than during the rest of life. The excitement of the artist at the easel or the scientist in the lab comes close to the ideal fulfillment we all hope to get from life, and so rarely do. Perhaps only sex, sports, music, and religious ecstasy—even when these experiences remain fleeting and leave no trace—provide as profound a sense of being part of an entity greater than ourselves. But creativity also leaves an outcome that adds to the richness and complexity of the future. An excerpt from one of the interviews on which this book is based may give a concrete idea of the joy involved in the creative endeavor, as well as the risks and hardships involved. The speaker is Vera Rubin, an astronomer who has contributed greatly to our knowledge about the dynamics of galaxies. She describes her recent discovery that stars belonging to a galaxy do not all rotate in the same direction; the orbits can circle either clockwise or counterclockwise on the same galactic plane. As is the case with many discoveries, this one was not planned. It was the result of an accidental observation of two pictures of the spectral analysis of the same galaxy obtained a year apart. By comparing the faint spectral lines indicating the positions of stars in the two pictures, Rubin noted that some had moved in one direction during the interval of time, and others had moved in the opposite direction. Rubin was lucky to be among the first cohort of astronomers to have access to such clear spectral analyses of nearby galaxies—a few years earlier, the details would not have been visible. But she could use this luck only because she had been, for years, deeply involved with the small details of the movements of stars. The finding was possible because the astronomer was interested in galaxies for their own sake, not because she wanted to prove a theory or make a name for herself. Here is her story: It takes a lot of courage to be a research scientist. It really does. I mean, you invest an enormous amount of yourself, your life, your time, and nothing may come of it. You could spend five years working on a problem and it could be wrong before you are done. Or someone might make a discovery just as you are finishing that could make it all wrong. That's a very real possibility. I guess I have been lucky. Initially I went into this [career] feeling very much that my role as an astronomer, as an observer, was just to gather very good data. I just looked upon my role as that of gathering valuable data for the astronomical community, and in most cases it turned out to be more than that. I wouldn't be disappointed if it were only that. But discoveries are always nice. I just discovered something this spring that's enchanting, and I remember how fun it was. With one of the postdocs, a young fellow, I was making a study of galaxies in the Virgo cluster. This is the biggest large cluster near us. Well, what I've learned in looking at these nearby clusters is that, in fact, I have enjoyed very much learning the details of each galaxy. I mean, I have almost gotten more interested in just their [individual traits], because these galaxies are close to us—well, close to us on a universal scale. This is the first time that I have ever had a large sample of galaxies all of which were close enough so that I could see lots of little details, and I have found that very strange things are happening near the centers of many of these galaxies—very rapid rotations, little discs, all kinds of interesting things—I have sort of gotten hung up on these little interesting things. So, having studied and measured them all and trying to decide what to do because it was such a vast quantity of interesting data, I realized that some of them were more interesting than others for all kinds of reasons, which I won't go into. So I decided that I would write up first those that had the most interesting central properties (which really had nothing to do with why I started the program), and I realized that there were *twenty or thirty that were just very interesting, and I picked fourteen. I decided to write a paper on these fourteen interesting galaxies. They all have very rapidly rotating cores and lots of gas and other things.*

For most of human history, creativity was held to be a prerogative of supreme beings. Religions the world over are based on origin myths in which one or more gods shaped the heavens, the earth, and the waters. Somewhere along the line they also created men and women—puny, helpless things subject to the wrath of the gods. It was only very recently in the history of the human race that the tables were reversed: It was now men and women who were the creators and gods the figments of their imagination. Whether this started in Greece or China two and a half millennia ago, or in Florence two thousand years later, does not matter much. The fact is that it happened quite recently in the multimillion-year history of the race. So we switched our views of the relationship between gods and humans. It is not so difficult to see why this happened. When the first myths of creation arose, humans were indeed helpless, at the mercy of cold, hunger, wild beasts, and one another. They had no idea how to explain the great forces they saw around them—the rising and setting of the sun, the wheeling stars, the alternating seasons. Awe suffused their groping for a foothold in this mysterious world. Then, slowly at first, and with increasing speed in the last thousand years or so, we began to understand how things work—from microbes to planets, from the circulation of the blood to ocean tides—and humans no longer seemed so helpless after all. Great machines were built, energies harnessed, the entire face of the earth transformed by human craft and appetite. It is not surprising that as we ride the crest of evolution we have taken over the title of creator. Whether this transformation will help the human race or cause its downfall is not yet clear. It would help if we realized the awesome responsibility of this new role. The gods of the ancients, like Shiva, like Yehova, were both builders and destroyers. The universe endured in a precarious balance between their mercy and their wrath. The world we inhabit today also teeters between becoming either the lovely garden or the barren desert that our contrary impulses strive to bring about. The desert is likely to prevail if we ignore the potential for destruction our stewardship implies and go on abusing blindly our new-won powers. While we cannot foresee the eventual results of creativity—of the attempt to impose our desires on reality, to become the main power that decides the destiny of every form of life on the planet—at least we can try to understand better what this force is and how it works. Because for better or for worse, our future is now closely tied to human creativity. The result will be determined in large part by our dreams and by the struggle to make them real. This book, which attempts to bring together thirty years of research on how creative people live and work, is an effort to make more understandable the mysterious process by which men and women come up with new ideas and new things. My work in this area has convinced me that creativity cannot be understood by looking only at the people who appear to make it happen. Just as the sound of a tree crashing in the forest is unheard if nobody is there to hear it, so creative ideas vanish unless there is a receptive audience to record and implement them. And without the assessment of competent outsiders, there is no reliable way to decide whether the claims of a self-styled creative person are valid. According to this view, creativity results from the interaction of a system composed of three elements: a culture that contains symbolic rules, a person who brings novelty into the symbolic domain, and a field of experts who recognize and validate the innovation. All three are necessary for a creative idea, product, or discovery to take place. For instance, in Vera Rubin's account of her astronomical discovery, it is impossible to imagine it without access to the huge amount of information about celestial motions that has been collecting for centuries, without access to the institutions that control modern large telescopes, without the critical skepticism and eventual support of other astronomers. In my view these are not incidental contributors to individual originality but essential components of the creative process, on a par with the individual's own contributions. For this reason, in this book I devote almost as much attention to the domain and to the field as to the individual creative persons. Creativity is the cultural equivalent of the process of genetic changes that result in biological evolution, where random variations take place in the chemistry of our chromosomes, below the threshold of consciousness. These changes result in the sudden appearance of a new physical characteristic in a child, and if the trait is an improvement over what existed before, it will have a greater chance to be transmitted to the child's descendants. Most new traits do not improve survival chances and may disappear after a few generations. But a few do, and it is these that account for biological evolution. In cultural evolution there are no mechanisms equivalent to genes and chromosomes. Therefore, a new idea or invention is not automatically passed on to the next generation. Instructions for how to use fire, or the wheel, or atomic energy are not built into the nervous *system of the children born after such discoveries. Each child has to learn them again from the start. The analogy to genes in the evolution of culture are memes, or units of information that we must learn if culture is to continue. Languages, numbers, theories, songs, recipes, laws, and values are all memes that we pass on to our children so that they will be remembered. It is these memes that a creative person changes, and if enough of the right people see the change as an improvement, it will become part of the culture. Therefore, to understand creativity it is not enough to study the individuals who seem most responsible for a novel idea or a new thing. Their contribution, while necessary and important, is only a link in a chain, a phase in a process. To say that Thomas Edison invented electricity or that Albert Einstein discovered relativity is a convenient simplification. It satisfies our ancient predilection for stories that are easy to comprehend and involve superhuman heroes. But Edison's or Einstein's discoveries would be inconceivable without the prior knowledge, without the intellectual and social network that stimulated their thinking, and without the social mechanisms that recognized and spread their innovations. To say that the theory of relativity was created by Einstein is like saying that it is the spark that is responsible for the fire. The spark is necessary, but without air and tinder there would be no flame. This book is not about the neat things children often say, or the creativity all of us share just because we have a mind and we can think. It does not deal with great ideas for clinching business deals, new ways for baking stuffed artichokes, or original ways of decorating the living room for a party. These are examples of creativity with a small c, which is an important ingredient of everyday life, one that we definitely should try to enhance. But to do so well it is necessary first to understand Creativity—and that is what this book tries to accomplish. ATTENTION AND CREATIVITY Creativity, at least as I deal with it in this book, is a process by which a symbolic domain in the culture is changed. New songs, new ideas, new machines are what creativity is about. But because these changes do not happen automatically as in biological evolution, it is necessary to consider the price we must pay for creativity to occur. It takes effort to change traditions. For example, memes must be learned before they can be changed: A musician must learn the musical tradition, the notation system, the way instruments are played before she can think of writing a new song; before an inventor can improve on airplane design he has to learn physics, aerodynamics, and why birds don't fall out of the sky. If we want to learn anything, we must pay attention to the information to be learned. And attention is a limited resource: There is just so much information we can process at any given time. Exactly how much we don't know, but it is clear that, for instance, we cannot learn physics and music at the same time. Nor can we learn well while we do the other things that need to be done and require attention, like taking a shower, dressing, cooking breakfast, driving a car, talking to our spouse, and so forth. The point is, a great deal of our limited supply of attention is committed to the tasks of surviving from one day to the next. Over an entire lifetime, the amount of attention left over for learning a symbolic domain—such as music or physics—is a fraction of this already small amount. Some important consequences follow logically from these simple premises. To achieve creativity in an existing domain, there must be surplus attention available. This is why such centers of creativity as Greece in the fifth century B.C., Florence in the fifteenth century, and Paris in the nineteenth century tended to be places where wealth allowed individuals to learn and to experiment above and beyond what was necessary for survival. It also seems true that centers of creativity tend to be at the intersection of different cultures, where beliefs, lifestyles, and knowledge mingle and allow individuals to see new combinations of ideas with greater ease. In cultures that are uniform and rigid, it takes a greater investment of attention to achieve new ways of thinking. In other words, creativity is more likely in places where new ideas require less effort to be perceived. As cultures evolve, it becomes increasingly difficult to master more than one domain of knowledge. Nobody knows who the last Renaissance man really was, but sometime after Leonardo da Vinci it became impossible to learn enough about all of the arts and the sciences to be an expert in more than a small fraction of them. Domains have split into subdomains, and a mathematician who has mastered algebra may not know much about number theory, combinatorix, topology—and vice versa. Whereas in the past an artist typically painted, sculpted, cast gold, and designed buildings, now all of these special skills tend to be acquired by different people. Therefore, it follows that as culture evolves, specialized knowledge will be favored over generalized knowledge. To see why this must be so, let us assume that there are three persons, one who studies physics, one who studies music, and one who studies both. Other things being equal, the person who studies both music and physics will have to split his or her attention between two symbolic domains, while the other two can focus theirs exclusively on a single domain. Consequently, the two specialized individuals can learn their domains in greater depth, and their expertise will be preferred over that of the generalist. With time, specialists are bound to take over leadership and control of the various institutions of culture. Of course, this trend toward specialization is not necessarily a good thing. It can easily lead to a cultural fragmentation such as described in the biblical story of the building of the Tower of Babel. Also, as the rest of this book amply demonstrates, creativity generally involves crossing the boundaries of domains, so that, for instance, a chemist who adopts quantum mechanics from physics and applies it to molecular bonds can make a more substantive contribution to chemistry than one who stays exclusively within the bounds of chemistry. Yet at the same time it is important to recognize that given how little attention we have to work with, and given the increasing amounts of information that are constantly being added to domains, specialization seems inevitable. This trend might be reversible, but only if we make a conscious effort to find an alternative; left to itself, it is bound to continue. Another consequence of limited attention is that creative individuals are often considered odd—or even arrogant, selfish, and ruthless. It is important to keep in mind that these are not traits of creative people, but traits that the rest of us attribute to them on the basis of our perceptions. When we meet a person who focuses all of his attention on physics or music and ignores us and forgets our names, we call that person "arrogant" even though he may be extremely humble and friendly if he could only spare attention from his pursuit. If that person is so taken with his domain that he fails to take our wishes into account we call him "insensitive" or "selfish" even though such attitudes are far from his mind. Similarly, if he pursues his work regardless of other people's plans, we call him "ruthless." Yet it is practically impossible to learn a domain deeply enough to make a change in it without dedicating all of one's attention to it and thereby appearing to be arrogant, selfish, and ruthless to those who believe they have a right to the creative person's attention. In fact, creative people are neither single-minded, specialized, nor selfish. Indeed, they seem to be the opposite: They love to make connections with adjacent areas of knowledge. They tend to be—in principle—caring and sensitive. Yet the demands of their role inevitably push them toward specialization and selfishness. Of the many paradoxes of creativity, this is perhaps the most difficult to avoid. WHAT'S THE GOOD OF STUDYING CREATIVITY? There are two main reasons why looking closely at the lives of creative individuals and the contexts of their accomplishments is useful. The first is the most obvious one: The results of creativity enrich the* culture and so they indirectly improve the quality of all our lives. But we may also learn from this knowledge how to make our own lives directly more interesting and productive. In the last chapter of this volume I summarize what this study suggests for enriching anyone's everyday existence. Some people argue that studying creativity is an elite distraction from the more pressing problems confronting us. We should focus all our energies on combating overpopulation, poverty, or mental retardation instead. A concern for creativity is an unnecessary luxury, according to this argument. But this position is somewhat shortsighted. First of all, workable new solutions to poverty or overpopulation will not appear magically by themselves. Problems are solved only when we devote a great deal of attention to them and in a creative way. Second, to have a good life, it is not enough to remove what is wrong from it. We also need a positive goal, otherwise why keep going? Creativity is one answer to that question: It provides one of the most exciting models for living. Psychologists have learned much about how healthy human beings think and feel from studying pathological cases. Brain-damaged patients, neurotics, and delinquents have provided contrasts against which normal functioning may better be understood. But we have learned little from the other end of the continuum, from people who are extraordinary in some positive sense. Yet if we wish to find out what might be missing from our lives, it makes sense to study lives that are rich and fulfilling. This is one of the main reasons for writing the book: to understand better a way of being that is more satisfying than most lives typically are. Each of us is born with two contradictory sets of instructions: a conservative tendency, made up of instincts for self-preservation, selfaggrandizement, and saving energy, and an expansive tendency made up of instincts for exploring, for enjoying novelty and risk—the curiosity that leads to creativity belongs to this set. We need both of these programs. But whereas the first tendency requires little encouragement or support from outside to motivate behavior, the second can wilt if it is not cultivated. If too few opportunities for curiosity are available, if too many obstacles are placed in the way of risk and exploration, the motivation to engage in creative behavior is easily extinguished. You would think that given its importance, creativity would have a high priority among our concerns. And in fact there is a lot of lip service paid to it. But if we look at the reality, we see a different picture. Basic scientific research is minimized in favor of immediate practical applications. The arts are increasingly seen as dispensable luxuries that must prove their worth in the *impersonal mass market. In one company after another, as downsizing continues, one hears CEOs report that this is not an age for innovators but for bookkeepers, not a climate for building and risking but for cutting expenses. Yet as economic competition heats up around the globe, exactly the opposite strategy is needed. And what holds true for the sciences, the arts, and for the economy also applies to education. When school budgets tighten and test scores wobble, more and more schools opt for dispensing with frills—usually with the arts and extracurricular activities—so as to focus instead on the so-called basics. This would not be bad if the "three Rs" were taught in ways that encouraged originality and creative thinking; unfortunately, they rarely are. Students generally find the basic academic subjects threatening or dull; their chance of using their minds in creative ways comes from working on the student paper, the drama club, or the orchestra. So if the next generation is to face the future with zest and self-confidence, we must educate them to be original as well as competent.*

Contents

1

Where Is Your Creativity

The answer is obvious: Creativity is some sort of mental activity, an insight that occurs inside the heads of some special people. But this short assumption is misleading. If by creativity we mean an idea or action that is new and valuable, then we cannot simply accept a person's own account as the criterionforitsexistenceThereis criterion for its existence. There is no way to know whether a thought is new except with reference to some standards, and there is no way to tell whether it is valuable until it passes social evaluation. Therefore, creativity does not happen inside people's heads, but in the interaction between a person's thoughts and a sociocultural context. It is a systemic rather than an individual phenomenon. Some examples will illustrate what I mean. When I was a graduate student I worked part-time for a few years as aneditorforaChicagopublishing an editor for a Chicago publishing house. At least once a week we would get in the mail a manuscript from an unknown author who claimed to have made a great discovery of one sort or another. Perhaps it was an eight-hundredpage tome that described in minute detail how a textual analysis of the Odyssey showed that, contrary to received opinion, Ulysses did not sail around the Mediterranean. Instead, according to the author's calculations, if one paid attention to the landmarks, the distances traveled, and the pattern of the stars mentioned by Homer, it was obviousthatUlyssesactually obvious that Ulysses actually traveled around the coast of Florida. Or it might be a textbook for building flying saucers, with extremely precise blueprints— which on closer inspection turned out to be copied from a service manual for a household appliance. What made reading these manuscripts depressing was the fact that their authors actually believed they had found something new and important and that their creative efforts went unrecognized only because of a conspiracy on the part ofphilistineslikemyselfandthe of philistines like myself and the editors of *all the other publishing houses. Some years ago the scientific world was abuzz with the news that two chemists had achieved cold fusion in the laboratory. If true, this meant that something very similar to the perpetual motion machine—one of the oldest dreams of mankind— was about to be realized. After a few frenetic months during which laboratories around the world attempted to replicate the initial claims—some with apparent success, but most without—it becameincreasinglyclearthatthe became increasingly clear that the experiments on which the claims were based had been flawed. So the researchers who at first were hailed as the greatest creative scientists of the century became somewhat of an embarrassment to the scholarly establishment. Yet, as far as we know, they firmly believed that they were right and that their reputations had been ruined by jealous colleagues. Jacob Rabinow, himself an inventor but also an evaluator of inventions for the National Bureau of Standards in Washington, has manysimilarstoriestotellabout many similar stories to tell about people who think they have invented perpetual motion machines: I've met many of these inventors who invent something that cannot work, that is theoretically impossible. But they spent three years developing it, running a motor without electricity, with magnets. You explain to them it won't work. It violates the second law of thermodynamics. And they say, "Don't give me your goddamn Washington laws." Who is right: the individual who believesinhisorherown believes in his or her own creativity, or the social milieu that denies it? If we take sides with the individual, then creativity becomes a subjective phenomenon. All it takes to be creative, then, is an inner assurance that what I think or do is new and valuable. There is nothing wrong with defining creativity this way, as long as we realize that this is not at all what the term originally was supposed to mean—namely, to bring into existence something genuinely new that is valued enough to be added to the culture. On the other hand, if we decide that social confirmation is necessaryforsomethingtobe necessary for something to be called creative, the definition must encompass more than the individual. What counts then is whether the inner certitude is validated by the appropriate experts —such as the editors of the publishing house in the case of farout manuscripts, or other scientists in the case of cold fusion. And it isn't possible to take a middle ground and say that sometimes the inner conviction is enough, while in other cases we need external confirmation. Such a compromise leaves a huge loophole, and trying to agree on whether something is creativeornotbecomes creative or not becomes impossible. The problem is that the term "creativity" as commonly used covers too much ground. It refers to very different entities, thus causing a great deal of confusion. To clarify the issues, I distinguish at least three different phenomena that can legitimately be called by that name. The first usage, widespread in ordinary conversation, refers to persons who express unusual thoughts, who are interesting and stimulating—in short, to people whoappeartobeunusuallybright who appear to be unusually bright. A brilliant conversationalist, a person with varied interests and a quick mind, may be called creative in this sense. Unless they also contribute something of permanent significance, I refer to people of this sort as brilliant rather than creative—and by and large I don't say much about them in this book. The second way the term can be used is to refer to people who experience the world in novel and original ways. These are individuals whose perceptions are fresh, whose judgments are insightfulwhomaymakeimportant insightful, who may make important discoveries that only they know about. I refer to such people as personally creative, and try to deal with them as much as possible (especially in chapter 14, which is devoted to this topic). But given the subjective nature of this form of creativity, it is difficult to deal with it no matter how important it is for those who experience it. The final use of the term designates individuals who, like Leonardo, Edison, Picasso, or Einstein, have changed our culture in some important respect. They are thecreativeoneswithout the creative ones without qualifications. Because their achievements are by definition public, it is easier to write about them, and the persons included in my study belong to this group. The difference among these three meanings is not just a matter of degree. The last kind of creativity is not simply a more developed form of the first two. These are actually different ways of being creative, each to a large measure unrelated to the others. It happens very often, for example, that some persons brimming with brilliance, whom everyonethinksofasbeing everyone thinks of as being exceptionally creative, never leave any accomplishment, any trace of their existence—except, perhaps, in the memories of those who have known them. Whereas some of the people who have had the greatest impact on history did not show any originality or brilliance in their behavior, except for the accomplishments they left behind. For example, Leonardo da Vinci, certainly one of the most creative persons in the third sense of the term, was apparently reclusive, and almost compulsive in his behavior. Ifyouhadmethimatacocktail If you had met him at a cocktail party, you would have thought that he was a tiresome bore and would have left him standing in a corner as soon as possible. Neither Isaac Newton nor Thomas Edison would have been considered assets at a party either, and outside of their scientific concerns they appeared colorless and driven. The biographers of outstanding creators struggle valiantly to make their subjects interesting and brilliant, yet more often than not their efforts are in vain. The accomplishments of a Michelangelo, a*

Beethoven, a Picasso, or an Einstein are awesomeintheirrespectivefields awesome in their respective fields —but their private lives, their everyday ideas and actions, would seldom warrant another thought were it not that their specialized accomplishments made everything they said or did of interest. By the definition I am using here, one of the most creative persons in this study is John Bardeen. He is the first person to have been awarded the Nobel prize in physics twice. The first time it was for developing the transistor; the second for his work on superconductivity. Few persons have ranged as widely and deeplyintherealmofsolidstate deeply in the realm of solid state physics, or come out with such important insights. But talking with Bardeen on any issue besides his work was not easy; his mind followed abstract paths while he spoke slowly, haltingly, and without much depth or interest about "real life" topics. It is perfectly possible to make a creative contribution without being brilliant or personally creative, just as it is possible—even likely—that someone personally creative will never contribute a thing to the culture. All three kinds of creativity enrichlifebymakingitmore enrich life by making it more interesting and fulfilling. But in this context I focus primarily on the third use of the term, and explore what is involved in the kind of creativity that leaves a trace in the cultural matrix. To make things more complicated, consider two more terms that are sometimes used interchangeably with creativity. The first is talent. Talent differs from creativity in that it focuses on an innate ability to do something very well. We might say that Michael Jordan is a talented athlete, or that Mozart was a talentedpianistwithoutimplying talented pianist, without implying that either was creative for that reason. In our sample, some individuals were talented in mathematics or in music, but the majority achieved creative results without any exceptional talent being evident. Of course, talent is a relative term, so it might be argued that in comparison to "average" individuals the creative ones are talented. The other term that is often used as a synonym for "creative" is genius. Again, there is an overlap. Perhaps we should think of a genius asapersonwhoisbothbrilliant as a person who is both brilliant and creative at the same time. But certainly a person can change the culture in significant ways without being a genius. Although several of the people in our sample have been called a genius by the media, they—and the majority of creative individuals we interviewed—reject this designation. THE SYSTEMS MODEL We have seen that creativity with a capital C, the kind that changes some aspect of the culture, is never only in the mind of a person. That wouldbydefinitionnotbeacaseof would by definition not be a case of cultural creativity. To have any effect, the idea must be couched in terms that are understandable to others, it must pass muster with *the experts in the field, and finally it must be included in the cultural domain to which it belongs. So the first question I ask of creativity is not what is it but where is it? The answer that makes most sense is that creativity can be observed only in the interrelations of a system made up of three main parts. The first of these is the domain, which consists of a set of symbolic rules and procedures Mathematics is a and procedures. Mathematics is a domain, or at a finer resolution algebra and number theory can be seen as domains. Domains are in turn nested in what we usually call culture, or the symbolic knowledge shared by a particular society, or by humanity as a whole. The second component of creativity is the field, which includes all the individuals who act as gatekeepers to the domain. It is their job to decide whether a new idea or product should be included in the domain. In the visual arts the field consists of art teachers, curators of museums collectors of curators of museums, collectors of art, critics, and administrators of foundations and government agencies that deal with culture. It is this field that selects what new works of art deserve to be recognized, preserved, and remembered. Finally, the third component of the creative system is the individual person. Creativity occurs when a person, using the symbols of a given domain such as music, engineering, business, or mathematics, has a new idea or sees a new pattern, and when this novelty is selected by the appropriate field for inclusion into appropriate field for inclusion into the relevant domain. The next generation will encounter that novelty as part of the domain they are exposed to, and if they are creative, they in turn will change it further. Occasionally creativity involves the establishment of a new domain: It could be argued that Galileo started experimental physics and that Freud carved psychoanalysis out of the existing domain of neuropathology. But if Galileo and Freud had not been able to enlist followers who came together in distinct fields to further their respective domains, their ideas would have had much less of ideas would have had much less of an impact, or none at all. So the definition that follows from this perspective is: Creativity is any act, idea, or product that changes an existing domain, or that transforms an existing domain into a new one. And the definition of a creative person is: someone whose thoughts or actions change a domain, or establish a new domain. It is important to remember, however, that a domain cannot be changed without the explicit or implicit consent of a field responsible for it. Several consequences follow from this way of looking at things. For instance, we don't need to assume that the creative person is necessarily different from anyone else. In other words, a personal trait of "creativity" is not what determines whether a person will be creative. What counts is whether the novelty he or she produces is accepted for inclusion in the domain. This may be the result of chance, perseverance, or being at the right place at the right time. Because creativity is jointly constituted by the interaction among domainfieldandpersonthetrait domain, field, and person, the trait of personal creativity may help generate the novelty that will change a domain, but it is neither a sufficient nor a necessary condition for it. A person cannot be creative in a domain to which he or she is not exposed. No matter how enormous mathematical gifts a child may have, he or she will not be able to contribute to mathematics without learning its rules. But even if the rules are learned, creativity cannot be manifested in the absence of a field that recognizes and legitimizes thenovelcontributionsAchild the novel contributions. A child might possibly learn mathematics on his or her own by finding the right books and the right mentors, but cannot make a difference in the domain unless recognized by teachers and journal editors who will witness to the appropriateness of the contribution. It also follows that creativity can be manifested only in existing domains and fields. For instance, it is very difficult to say "This woman is very creative at nurturing" or "This woman is very creative in her wisdom," because nurturance and wisdomalthoughextremely wisdom, although extremely important for human survival, are loosely organized domains with few generally accepted rules and priorities, and they lack a field of experts who can determine the legitimacy of claims. So we are in the paradoxical situation that novelty is more obvious in domains that are often relatively trivial but easy to measure; whereas in domains that are more essential novelty is very difficult to determine. There can be agreement on whether a new computer game, rock song, or economic formula is actually novel, and therefore creativelesseasytoagreeonthe creative, less easy to agree on the novelty of an act of compassion or of an insight into human nature. The model also allows for the often mysterious fluctuations in the attribution of creativity over time. For example, the reputation of Raphael as a painter has waxed and waned several times since his heyday at the court of Pope Julius II. Gregor Mendel did not become famous as the creator of experimental genetics until half a century after his death. Johann Sebastian Bach's music was dismissed as old-fashioned for severalgenerationsThe several generations. The conventional explanation is that Raphael, Mendel, and Bach were always creative, only their reputation changed with the vagaries of social recognition. But the systems model recognizes the fact that creativity cannot be separated from its recognition. Mendel was not creative during his years of relative obscurity because his experimental findings were not that important until a group of British geneticists, at the end of the nineteenth century, recognized their implications for evolution. The creativity of Raphael fluctuatesasarthistorical fluctuates as art historical knowledge, art critical theories, and the aesthetic sensitivity of the age change. According to the systems model, it makes perfect sense to say that Raphael was creative in the sixteenth and in the nineteenth centuries but not in between or afterward. Raphael is creative when the community is moved by his work, and discovers new possibilities in his paintings. But when his paintings seem mannered and routine to those who know art, Raphael can only be called a great draftsman, a subtle colorist— perhaps even a personally creative individualbutnotcreativewitha individual—but not creative with a capital C. If creativity is more than personal insight and is cocreated by domains, fields, and persons, then creativity can be constructed, deconstructed, and reconstructed several times over the course of history. Here is one of our respondents, the poet Anthony Hecht, commenting on this issue: Literary reputations are constantly shifting. Sometimes in trifling, frivolous ways. There was a former colleague of mine who, at a recent meeting of the English Department, said that she thoughtitwasnownolonger thought it was now no longer important to teach Shakespeare because among other things he had a very feeble grasp of women. Now that seems to me as trifling an observation as can be made, but it does mean that, if you take this seriously, nobody's place in the whole canon is very secure, that it's constantly changing. And this is both good and bad. John Donne's position was in the nineteenth century of no consequence at all. The Oxford Book of English Verse had only one poem of his. And now, of course, he was resurrected by HerbertGriersonandTSEliot Herbert Grierson and T. S. Eliot and he's one of the great figures of seventeenth-century poetry. But he wasn't always. This is true of music, too. Bach was eclipsed for two hundred years and rediscovered by Mendelssohn. This means that we are constantly reassessing the past. And that's a good, valuable, and indeed necessary thing to do. This way of looking at things might seem insane to some. The usual way to think about this issue is that someone like van Gogh was a great creative genius, but his contemporariesdidnotrecognize contemporaries did not recognize this. Fortunately, now we have discovered what a great painter he was after all, so his creativity has been vindicated. Few flinch at the presumption implicit in such a view. What we are saying is that we know what great art is so much better than van Gogh's contemporaries did—those bourgeois philistines. What— besides unconscious conceit— warrants this belief? A more objective description of van Gogh's contribution is that his creativity came into being when a sufficient number of art experts felt that his paintingshadsomethingimportant paintings had something important to contribute to the domain of art. Without such a response, van Gogh would have remained what he was, a disturbed man who painted strange canvases. Perhaps the most important implication of the systems model is that the level of creativity in a given place at a given time does not depend only on the amount of individual creativity. It depends just as much on how well suited the respective domains and fields are to the recognition and diffusion of novel ideas. This can make a great dealofpracticaldifferenceto deal of practical difference to efforts for enhancing creativity. Today many American corporations spend a great deal of money and time trying to increase the originality of their employees, hoping thereby to get a competitive edge in the marketplace. But such programs make no difference unless management also learns to recognize the valuable ideas among the many novel ones, and then finds ways of implementing them. For instance, Robert Galvin at Motorola is justly concerned about the fact that in order to survive amongthehungryPacificRim among the hungry Pacific Rim electronic manufacturers, his company must make creativity an intentional part of its productive process. He is also right in perceiving that to do so he first has to encourage the thousands of engineers working for the company to generate as many novel ideas as possible. So various forms of brainstorming are instituted, where employees free-associate without fear of being ridiculously impractical. But the next steps are less clear. How does the field (in this case, management) choose among the multitude of new ideas theonesworthpursuing?Andhow the ones worth pursuing? And how can the chosen ideas be included in the domain (in this case, the production schedule of Motorola)? Because we are used to thinking that creativity begins and ends with the person, it is easy to miss the fact that the greatest spur to it may come from changes outside the individual. CREATIVITY IN THE RENAISSANCE A good example is the sudden spurt in artistic creativity that took place in Florence between 1400 and 1425. These were the golden years oftheRenaissanceanditis of the Renaissance, and it is generally agreed that some of the most influential new works of art in Europe were created during that quarter century. Any list of the masterpieces would include the dome of the cathedral built by Brunelleschi, the "Gates of Paradise" crafted for the baptistery by Ghiberti, Donatello's sculptures for the chapel of Orsanmichele, the fresco cycle by Masaccio in the Brancacci Chapel, and Gentile da Fabriano's painting of the Adoration of the Magi in the Church of the Trinity. How can this flowering of great artbeexplained?Ifcreativityis art be explained? If creativity is something entirely within a person, we would have to argue that for some reason an unusually large number of creative artists were born in Florence in the last decades of the fourteenth century. Perhaps some freak genetic mutation occurred, or a drastic change in the education of Florentine children suddenly caused them to become more creative. But an explanation involving the domain and the field is much more sensible. As far as the domain is concerned, the Renaissance was madepossibleinpartbythe made possible in part by the rediscovery of ancient Roman methods of building and sculpting that had been lost for centuries during the so-called Dark Ages. In Rome and elsewhere, by the end of the thirteen hundreds, eager scholars were excavating classical ruins, copying down and analyzing the styles and techniques of the ancients. This slow preparatory work bore fruit at the turn of the fifteenth century, opening up long forgotten knowledge to the artisans and craftsmen of the time. The cathedral of Florence, Santa MariaNovellahadbeenleftopen Maria Novella, had been left open to the skies for eighty years because no one could find a way to build a dome over its huge apse. There was no known method for preventing the walls from collapsing inward once the curvature of the dome had advanced beyond a certain height. Every year eager young artists and established builders submitted plans to the Opera del Duomo, the board that supervised the building of the cathedral, but their plans were found unpersuasive. The Opera was made up of the political and business leaders of the city, and their personal reputations were at stakeinthischoiceForeighty stake in this choice. For eighty years they did not feel that any proposed solution for the completion of the dome was worthy of the city, and of themselves. But eventually humanist scholars became interested in the Pantheon of Rome, measured its enormous dome, and analyzed how it had been constructed. The Pantheon had been rebuilt by the emperor Hadrian in the second century. The diameter of its 71-foot-high dome was 142 feet. Nothing on that scale had been built for well over a thousand years, and the methods that allowed the Romanstobuildsuchastructure Romans to build such a structure that would stand up and not collapse had been long forgotten in the dark centuries of barbarian invasions. But now that peace and commerce were reviving the Italian cities, the knowledge was slowly being pieced back together. Brunelleschi, who in 1401 appears to have visited Rome to study its antiquities, understood the importance of the studies of the Pantheon. His idea for how to complete the dome in Florence was based on the framework of internal stone arches that would help containthethrustandthe contain the thrust, and the herringbone brickwork between them. But his design was not just a restatement of the Roman model—it was influenced also by all the architecture of the intervening centuries, especially the Gothic models. When he presented his plan to the Opera, they recognized it as a feasible and beautiful solution. And after the dome was built, it became a liberating new form that inspired hundreds of builders who came after him, including Michelangelo, who based on it his design for the cupola of St. Peter's in Rome. But no matter how influential the rediscoveryofclassicalartforms* rediscovery of classical art forms, the Florentine Renaissance cannot be explained only in terms of the sudden availability of information. Otherwise, the same flowering of new artistic forms would have taken place in all the other cities exposed to the ancient models. And though this actually did happen to a certain extent, no other place matched Florence in the intensity and depth of artistic achievement. Why was this so? The explanation is that the field of art became particularly favorable to the creation of new works at just aboutthesametimeasthe about the same time as the rediscovery of the ancient domains of art. Florence had become one of the richest cities in Europe first through trading, then through the manufacture of wool and other textiles, and finally through the financial expertise of its rich merchants. By the end of the fourteenth century there were a dozen major bankers in the city— the Medici being only one of the minor ones—who were getting substantial interest every year from the various foreign kings and potentates to whom they had lent money. But while the coffers of the bankers were getting fuller, the city itself was troubled. Men without property were ruthlessly exploited, and political tensions fueled by economic inequality threatened at any moment to explode into open conflict. The struggle between pope and emperor, which divided the entire continent, was reproduced inside the city in the struggle between the Guelf and Ghibelline factions. To make matters worse, Florence was surrounded by Siena, Pisa, and Arezzo, cities jealous of its wealth and ambitions and alwaysreadytosnatchaway always ready to snatch away whatever they could of Florentine trade and territory. It was in this atmosphere of wealth and uncertainty that the urban leaders decided to invest in making Florence the most beautiful city in Christendom—in their words, "a new Athens." By building awesome churches, impressive bridges, and splendid palaces, and by commissioning great frescoes and majestic statues, they must have felt that they were weaving a protective spell around their homes and businesses. And in awaytheywerenotwrong:When a way, they were not wrong: When more than five hundred years later Hitler ordered the retreating German troops to blow up the bridges on the Arno and level the city around them, the field commander refused to obey on the grounds that too much beauty would be erased from the world—and the city was saved. The important thing to realize is that when the Florentine bankers, churchmen, and heads of great guilds decided to make their city intimidatingly beautiful, they did not just throw money at artists and wait toseewhathappenedTheybecame to see what happened. They became intensely involved in the process of encouraging, evaluating, and selecting the works they wanted to see completed. It was because the leading citizens, as well as the common people, were so seriously concerned *with the outcome of their work that the artists were pushed to perform beyond their previous limits. Without the constant encouragement and scrutiny of the members of the Opera, the dome over the cathedral would probably not have been as beautiful as it eventually turned out to be. Another illustration of how the fieldofartoperatedinFlorenceat field of art operated in Florence at this time concerns the building of the north and especially the east door of the baptistery, one of the uncontested masterpieces of the period, which Michelangelo declared was worthy of being the "Gate of Paradise" when he saw its heart-wrenching beauty. In this case also a special commission had been formed to supervise the building of the doors for this public edifice. The board was composed of eminent individuals, mostly the leaders of the guild of wool weavers that was financing the project. The board decided that eachdoorshouldbeofbronzeand each door should be of bronze and have ten panels illustrating Old Testament themes. Then they wrote to some of the most eminent philosophers, writers, and churchmen in Europe to request their opinion of which scenes from the Bible should be included in the panels, and how they should be represented. After the answers came in, they drew up a list of specifications for the doors and in 1401 announced a competition for their design. From the dozens of drawings submitted the board chose five finalistsBrunelleschiand finalists—Brunelleschi and Ghiberti among them. The finalists on the short list were given a year to finish a bronze mock-up of one of the door panels. The subject was to be "The Sacrifice of Isaac" and had to include at least one angel and one sheep in addition to Abraham and his son. During that year all five finalists were paid handsomely by the board for time and materials. In 1402 the jury reconvened to consider the new entries and selected Ghiberti's panel, which showed technical excellence as well as a wonderfully natural yet classical composition. Lorenzo Ghiberti was twenty-one years old at the time. He spent the next twenty years finishing the north door and then another twenty-seven finishing the famed east door. He was involved with perfecting the baptistery doors from 1402 to 1452, a span of a half century. Of course, in the meantime he finished many more commissions and sculpted statues for the Medicis, the Pazzis, the guild of merchant bankers, and other notables, but his reputation rests on the Gates of Paradise, which changed the Western world's conception of decorative art. If Brunelleschi had been influenced by Roman architecture, Ghiberti studied and tried to emulate Roman sculpture. He had to relearn the technique for casting large bronze shapes, and he studied the classic profiles carved on Roman tombs on which he modeled the expressions of the characters he made emerge from the door panels. And again, he combined the rediscovered classics with the more recent Gothic sculpture produced in Siena.*

However, one could claim without too much risk of exaggeration that what made the GatesofParadisesobeautifulwas Gates of Paradise so beautiful was the care, concern, and support of the entire community, represented by the field of judges who supervised their construction. If Ghiberti and his fellows were driven to surpass themselves, it was by the intense competition and focused attention their work attracted. Thus the sociologist of art Arnold Hauser rightly assesses this period: "In the art of the early Renaissance...the starting point of production is to be found mostly not in the creative urge, the subjective self-expression and spontaneous inspiration of the artist, but in the task set by the customer" customer." Of course, the great works of Florentine art would never have been made just because the domain of classical art had been rediscovered, or because the rulers of the city had decided to make it beautiful. Without individual artists the Renaissance could not have taken place. After all, it was Brunelleschi who built the dome over Santa Maria Novella, and it was Ghiberti who spent his life casting the Gates of Paradise. At the same time, it must be recognized that without previous models and thesupportofthecityBrunelleschi the support of the city, Brunelleschi and Ghiberti could not have done what they did. And that with the favorable conjunction of field and domain, if these two artists had not been born, some others would have stepped in their place and built the dome and the doors. It is because of this inseparable connection that creativity must, in the last analysis, be seen not as something happening within a person but in the relationships within a system. DOMAINS OF KNOWLEDGE AND ACTION It seems that every species of living organismexceptforushumans organism, except for us humans, understands the world in terms of more or less built-in responses to certain types of sensations. Plants turn toward the sun. There are amoebas sensitive to magnetic attraction that orient their bodies toward the North pole. Baby indigo buntings learn the patterns of the stars as they look out of their nests and then are able to fly great distances at night without losing their way. Bats respond to sounds, sharks to smell, and birds of prey have incredibly developed vision. Each species experiences and understands its environment in termsoftheinformationitssensory terms of the information its sensory equipment is programmed to process. The same is true for humans. But in addition to the narrow windows on the world our genes have provided, we have managed to open up new perspectives on reality based on information mediated by symbols. Perfect parallel lines do not exist in nature, but by postulating their existence Euclid and his followers could build a system for representing spatial relations that is much more precise than what the unaided eye and brain canachieveDifferentastheyare can achieve. Different as they are from each other, lyric poetry and magnetic resonance spectroscopy are both ways to make accessible information that otherwise we would never have an inkling about. Knowledge mediated by symbols is extrasomatic; it is not transmitted through the chemical codes inscribed in our chromosomes but must be intentionally passed on and learned. It is this extrasomatic information that makes up what we call a culture. And the knowledge conveyed by symbols is bundled up in discrete domains—geometry, musicreligionlegalsystemsand music, religion, legal systems, and so on. Each domain is made up of its own symbolic elements, its own rules, and generally has its own system of notation. In many ways, each domain describes an isolated little world in which a person can think and act with clarity and concentration. The existence of domains is perhaps the best evidence of human creativity. The fact that calculus and Gregorian chants exist means that we can experience patterns of order that were not programmed into our genes by biological evolution. By learningtherulesofadomainwe learning the rules of a domain, we immediately step beyond the boundaries of biology and enter the realm of cultural evolution. Each domain expands the limitations of individuality and enlarges our sensitivity and ability to relate to the world. Each person is surrounded by an almost infinite number of domains that are potentially able to open up new worlds and give new powers to those who learn their rules. Therefore, it is astounding how few of us bother to invest enough mental energy to learn the rules of even one of these domains, and live instead exclusivelywithintheconstraintsof exclusively within the constraints of biological existence. For most people, domains are primarily ways to make a living. We choose nursing or plumbing, medicine or business administration because of our ability and the chances of getting a well-paying job. But then there are individuals —and the creative ones are usually in this group—who choose certain domains because of a powerful calling to do so. For them the match is so perfect that acting within the rules of the domain is rewarding in itself; they would keep doing what theydoeveniftheywerenotpaid they do even if they were not paid for it, just for the sake of doing the activity. Despite the multiplicity of domains, there are some common reasons for pursuing them for their own sake. Nuclear physics, microbiology, poetry, and musical composition share few symbols and rules, yet the calling for these different domains is often astonishingly similar. To bring order to experience, to make something that will endure after one's death, to do something that allows humankind to go beyond its presentpowersareverycommon present powers are very common themes. When asked why he decided to become a poet at the age of seven, György Faludy answered, "Because I was afraid to die." He explained that creating patterns with words, patterns that because of their truth and beauty had a chance to survive longer than the body of the poet, was an act of defiance and hope that gave meaning and direction to his life for the next seventy-three years. This urge is not so very different from physicist John Bardeen's description of his work on superconductivitythatmightleadto superconductivity that might lead to a world without friction, the physicist Heinz Maier-Leibnitz's hope that nuclear energy will provide unlimited power, or the biochemical physicist Manfred Eigen's attempt to understand how life evolved. Domains are wonderfully different, but the human quest they represent converges on a few themes. In many ways, Max Planck's obsession with understanding the Absolute underlies most human attempts to transcend the limitations of a body doomed to die after a short span of years. There are several ways that domains can help or hinder creativity. Three major dimensions are particularly relevant: the clarity of structure, the centrality within the culture, and accessibility. Say that pharmaceutical companies A and B are competing in the same market. The amount of money they devote to research and development, as well as the creative potential of their researchers, is equal. Now we want to predict whether company A or B will come up with the most effective new drugs, basing our prediction solely on domain characteristicsThequestionswe characteristics. The questions we would ask are the following: Which company has the more detailed data about pharmaceuticals? Where are the data better organized? Which company puts more emphasis in its culture on research, relative to other areas such as production and marketing? Where does pharmaceutical knowledge earn more respect? Which company disseminates knowledge better among its staff? Where is it easier to test a hypothesis? The company where knowledge is better structured, more central, and more accessible is likely to be the one whereotherthingsstillbeing where—other things still being equal—creative innovations are going to happen. It has been often remarked that superior ability in some domains— such as mathematics or music— shows itself earlier in life than in other domains—such as painting or philosophy. Similarly, it has been suggested that the most creative performances in some domains are the work of young people, while in other domains older persons have the edge. The most creative lyric verse is believed to be that written by the young, while epics tend to be writtenbymorematurepoets written by more mature poets. Mathematical genius peaks in the twenties, physics in the thirties, but great philosophical works are usually achieved later in life. The most likely explanation for these differences lies in the different ways these domains are structured. The symbolic system of mathematics is organized relatively tightly; the internal logic is strict; the system maximizes clarity and lack of redundancy.

Therefore, it is easy for a young person to assimilate the rules quickly and jump to the cutting edge of the domaininafewyearsForthesame domain in a few years. For the same structural reasons, when a novelty is proposed—like the long-awaited proof of Fermat's last theorem presented by a relatively young mathematician in 1993—it is immediately recognized and, if viable, accepted. By contrast, it takes decades for social scientists or philosophers to master their domains, and if they produce a new idea, it takes the field many years to assess whether it is an improvement worth adding to the knowledge base. Heinz Maier-Leibnitz tells the storyofasmallphysicsseminarhe story of a small physics seminar he taught in Munich, which was interrupted one day by a graduate student who suggested a new way to represent on the blackboard the behavior of a subatomic particle. The professor agreed that the new formulation was an improvement and praised the student for having thought of it. By the end of the week, Maier-Leibnitz says, he started getting calls from physicists at other German universities, asking in effect, "Is it true that one of your students came up with such and such an idea?" The next week, calls began to come in from American universitiesontheEastCoastIn universities on the East Coast. In two weeks, colleagues from Cal Tech, Berkeley, and Stanford were asking the same question. This story could never have been told about my branch of psychology. If a student stood up in a psychology seminar at any school in the world and uttered the most profound ideas, he or she would not create a ripple beyond the walls of the classroom. Not because psychology students are less intelligent or original than the ones in physics. Nor because my colleagues and I are less alert to ourstudents'newideasBut our students' new ideas. But because with the exception of a few highly structured subdomains, psychology is so diffuse a system of thought that it takes years of intense writing for any person to say something that others recognize as new and important. The young student in Maier-Leibnitz's class was eventually awarded the Nobel Prize in physics, something that could never happen to a psychologist. Does this mean that a domain that is better structured—where creativity is easier to determine—is insomesense"better"thanonethat in some sense "better" than one that is more diffuse? That it is more important, more advanced, more serious? Not at all. If that were true, then chess, microeconomics, or computer programming, which are very clearly structured domains, would have to be considered more advanced than morality or wisdom. But it is certainly true that nowadays a quantifiable domain with sharp boundaries and welldefined rules is taken more seriously. In a typical university it is much easier to get funding for such a department. It is also easier tojustifypromotionforateacherin to justify promotion for a teacher in a narrowly defined domain: Ten colleagues will willingly write letters of recommendation stating that professor X should be promoted because she is the world's authority on the mating habits of the kangaroo rat or on the use of the subjunctive in Dravidic languages. It is much less likely that ten scholars would agree on who is a world authority on personality development. From this it is easy to make the regrettable mistake of inferring that personality development is a scientifically less respectable domain than the one that studiesthematingpracticesofthe studies the mating practices of the kangaroo rat. In the current historical climate, a domain where quantifiable measurement is possible takes precedence over one where it does not. We believe that things that can be measured are real, and we ignore those that we don't know how to measure. So people take intelligence very seriously, because the mental ability we call by that name can be measured by tests; whereas few bother about how sensitive, altruistic, or helpful someone is, because as yet there is nogoodwaytomeasuresuch no good way to measure such qualities. Sometimes this bias has profound consequences—for instance, in how we define social progress and achievement. One of futurist Hazel Henderson's life goals is to convince world governments to start computing less easily measured trends in their Gross Natural Product. As long as the costs of pollution, depredation of natural resources, decline in the quality of life, and various other human costs are left out of the reckoning of the GNP, she claims, entirely distorted pictures of reality result. A country may pride itself on allitsnewhighwayswhilethe all its new highways while the resulting auto emissions are causing widespread emphysema. FIELDS OF ACCOMPLISHMENT If a symbolic domain is necessary for a person to innovate in, a field is necessary to determine whether the innovation is worth making a fuss about. Only a very small percentage of the great number of novelties produced will eventually become part of the culture. For instance, about one hundred thousand new books are published every year in the United States. Howmanyofthesewillbe How many of these will be remembered ten years from now? Similarly, about five hundred thousand people in this country state on their census forms that they are artists. If each of them painted only one picture a year, it would amount to about fifteen million new paintings per generation. How many of these will end up in museums or in textbooks on art? One in a million, ten in a million, one in ten thousand? One? George Stigler, the Nobel laureate in economics, made the same point about new ideas produced in his domainandwhathesayscanbe domain, and what he says can be applied to any other field of science: The profession is too busy to read much. I keep telling my colleagues at the Journal of Political Economy that anytime we get an article that fifteen of our profession, of the seven thousand subscribers, *read carefully, that must be truly a major article of the year. These numbers suggest that the competition between memes, or units of cultural information, is as fierceasthecompetitionbetween fierce as the competition between the units of chemical information we call genes. In order to survive, cultures must eliminate most of the new ideas their members produce. Cultures are conservative, and for good reason. No culture could assimilate all the novelty people produce without dissolving into chaos. Suppose you had to pay equal attention to the fifteen million paintings—how much time would you have left free to eat, sleep, work, or listen to music? In other words, no person can afford to pay attention to more than a very small fraction of new things produced. Yetaculturecouldnotsurvivelong Yet a culture could not survive long unless all of its members paid attention to at least a few of the same things. In fact it could be said that a culture exists when the majority of people agree that painting X deserves more attention than painting Y, or idea X deserves more thought than idea Y. Because of the scarcity of attention, we must be selective: We remember and recognize only a few of the works of art produced, we read only a few of the new books written, we buy only a few of the new appliances busily being inventedUsuallyitisthevarious invented. Usually it is the various fields that act as filters to help us select among the flood of new information those memes worth paying attention to. A field is made up of experts in a given domain whose job involves passing judgment on performance in that domain. Members of the field choose from among the novelties those that deserve to be included in the canon. This competition also means that a creative person must convince the field that he or she has made a valuable innovation. This is never aneasytaskStigleremphasizesthe an easy task. Stigler emphasizes the necessity of this difficult struggle for recognition: I think you have to accept the judgment of others. Because if one were allowed to judge his own case, every one of us should have been president of the United States and received all the medals and so forth. And so I guess I am most proud of the things in which I succeeded in impressing other people with what I have done. And those would be things like the two areas of work in which I received the Nobel Prize, and thingslikethatSothoseand things like that. So those and certain other works that my profession has liked would be, as far as my professional life goes, the things of which I'm most proud. I have always looked upon the task of a scientist as bearing the responsibility for persuading his contemporaries of the cogency and validity of his thinking. He isn't entitled to a warm reception. He has to earn it, whether by the skill of his exposition, the novelty of his ideas, or what. I've written on subjects which I thought had promisewhichhaven'tamounted promise which haven't amounted* to much. That's all right. That may well mean that my judgment wasn't good, because I don't think any one person's judgment is as good as that of a collection of his better colleagues. Fields vary greatly in terms of how specialized versus how inclusive they are. For some domains, the field is as broad as society itself. It took the entire population of the United States to decide whether the recipe for New Coke was an innovation worth keeping. On the other hand, it has beensaidthatonlyfourorfive been said that only four or five people in the world initially understood Einstein's theory of relativity, but their opinion had enough weight to make his name a household word. But even in Einstein's case, the broader society had a voice in deciding that his work deserved a central place in our culture. To what extent, for instance, did his fame depend on the fact that he looked like a scientist from Hollywood central casting? That he was persecuted by our enemies, the Nazis? That many interpreted his discoveries as supportive of the relativity of valuesandthusofferinga values, and thus offering a refreshing alternative to binding social norms and beliefs? That while yearning to overthrow old beliefs, we also thirst for new certainties, and Einstein was said to have come up with an important new truth? Although none of these considerations bears in the least on the theory of relativity, they were all very much part of how the media portrayed Einstein—and it is these traits rather than the profundity of his theory that presumably convinced most people that he was worth including in the cultural pantheon. Fields can affect the rate of creativity in at least three ways. The first way is by being either reactive or proactive. A reactive field does not solicit or stimulate novelty, while a proactive field does. One of the major reasons the Renaissance was so bountiful in Florence is that the patrons actively demanded novelty from artists. In the United States, we make some effort to be proactive in terms of stimulating scientific creativity in the young: science fairs and prestigious prizes like the Westinghouse, which goes to the onehundredbesthighschool one hundred best high school science projects each year, are some examples. But of course much more could be done to stimulate novel thinking in science early on. Similarly, some companies like Motorola take seriously the idea that one way to increase creativity is for the field to be proactive. The second way for the field to influence the rate of novelty is by choosing either a narrow or a broad filter in the selection of novelty. Some fields are conservative and allow only a few new items to enter the domain at any given time. They rejectmostnoveltyandselectonly reject most novelty and select only what they consider best. Others are more liberal in allowing new ideas into their domains, and as a result these change more rapidly. At the extremes, both strategies can be dangerous: It is possible to wreck a domain either by starving it of novelty or by admitting too much unassimilated novelty into it. Finally, fields can encourage novelty if they are well connected to the rest of the social system and are able to channel support into their own domain. For instance, after World War II it was easy for nuclearphysiciststogetallsortsof nuclear physicists to get all sorts of money to build new laboratories, research centers, experimental reactors, and to train new physicists, because politicians and voters were still enormously impressed by the atomic bomb and the future possibilities it represented. During a few years in the 1950s, the number of students in theoretical physics at the University of Rome went from seven to two hundred; the proportions were not so far off elsewhere around the world. There are several ways that domainsandfieldscanaffecteach domains and fields can affect each other. Sometimes domains determine to a large extent what the field can or cannot do; this is probably more usual in the sciences, where the knowledge base severely restricts what the scientific establishment can or cannot claim. No matter how much a group of scientists would like their pet theory accepted, it won't be if it runs against the previously accumulated consensus. In the arts, on the other hand, it is often the field that takes precedence: The artistic establishment decides, without firm guidelines anchored in thepastwhichnewworksofart the past, which new works of art are worthy of inclusion in the domain. Sometimes fields that are not competent in the domain take control over it. The church interfered in Galileo's astronomical findings; the Communist party for a while directed not only Soviet genetics but art and music as well; and fundamentalists in the United States are trying to have a voice in teaching evolutionary history. In more subtle ways, economic and political forces always influence, whether intentionally or not, the developmentofdomainsOur development of domains. Our knowledge of foreign languages would be even less if the U.S. government stopped subsidizing Title IV programs. Opera and ballet would virtually disappear without massive outside support. The Japanese government is heavily invested in stimulating new ideas and applications in micro-circuitry, while the Dutch government, understandably enough, encourages pioneering work in the building of dams and hydraulic devices. The Romanian government was actively involved in the destruction of the art forms of its ethnic minorities in ordertomaintainthepurityof order to maintain the purity of Dacian culture; the Nazis tried to destroy what they considered "degenerate" Jewish art. At times fields become unable to represent well a particular domain. A leading philosopher in our study maintains that if a young person wants to learn philosophy these days, he or she would be better advised to become immersed in the domain directly and avoid the field altogether: "I'd tell him to read the great books of philosophy. And I would tell him not to do graduate study at any university. I think all philosophydepartmentsareno philosophy departments are no good. They are all terrible." By and large, however, jurisdiction over a given domain is officially left in the hands of a field of experts. These may range from grade school teachers to university professors and include anyone who has a right to decide whether a new idea or product is "good" or "bad." It is impossible to understand creativity without understanding how fields operate, how they decide whether something new should or should not be added to the domain. THE CONTRIBUTIONS OF THE PERSON PERSON Finally we get to the individual responsible for generating novelty. Most investigations focus on the creative person, believing that by understanding how his or her mind works, the key to creativity will be found. But this is not necessarily the case. For though it is true that behind every new idea or product there is a person, it does not follow that such persons have a single characteristic responsible for the novelty. Perhaps being creative is more likebeinginvolvedinan like being involved in an automobile accident. There are some traits that make one more likely to be in an accident—being young and male, for instance—but usually we cannot explain car accidents on the basis of the driver's characteristics alone. There are too many other variables involved: the condition of the road, the other driver, the type of traffic, the weather, and so on. Accidents, like creativity, are properties of systems rather than of individuals. Nor can we say that it is the person who starts the creative processInthecaseofthe process. In the case of the Florentine Renaissance one could just as well say that it was started by the rediscovery of Roman art, or by the stimulation provided by the city's bankers. Brunelleschi and his friends found themselves in a stream of thought and action that started before they were born, and then they stepped into the middle of it. At first it appears that they initiated the great works that made the epoch famous, but in reality they were only catalysts for a much more complex process with many participants and many inputs. When we asked creative persons whatexplainstheirsuccessoneof what explains their success, one of the most frequent answers— perhaps the most frequent one— was that they were lucky. Being in the right place at the right time is an almost universal explanation. Several scientists who were in graduate school in the late 1920s or 1930s remember being among the first cohorts to be exposed to quantum theory. Inspired by the work of Max Planck and Niels Bohr, they applied quantum mechanics to chemistry, to biology, to astrophysics, to electrodynamics. Some of them, like Linus Pauling, John Bardeen, Manfred Eigen, SubrahmanyanChandrasekharwere Subrahmanyan Chandrasekhar, were awarded Nobel Prizes for extending the theory to new domains. Many women scientists who entered graduate school in the 1940s mention that they wouldn't *have been accepted by the schools, and certainly they wouldn't have been given fellowships and special attention from supervisors, except for the fact that there were so few male students left to compete against, most of them having gone to war. Luck is without doubt an important ingredient in creative discoveriesAverysuccessful discoveries. A very successful artist, whose work sells well and hangs in the best museums and who can afford a large estate with horses and a swimming pool, once admitted ruefully that there could be at least a thousand artists as good as he is—yet they are unknown and their work is unappreciated. The one difference between him and the rest, he said, was that years back he met at a party a man with whom he had a few drinks. They hit it off and became friends. The man eventually became a successful art dealer who did his best to push his friend's work. One thing led to another: A richcollectorbegantobuythe rich collector began to buy the artist's work, critics started paying attention, a large museum added one of his works to its permanent collection. And once the artist became successful, the field discovered his creativity. It is important to point out the tenuousness of the individual contribution to creativity, because it is usually so often overrated. Yet one can also fall in the opposite error and deny the individual any credit. Certain sociologists and social psychologists claim that creativity is all a matter of attributionThecreativepersonis attribution. The creative person is like a blank screen on which social consensus projects exceptional qualities. Because we need to believe that creative people exist, we endow some individuals with this illusory quality. This, too, is an oversimplification. For while the individual is not as important as it is commonly supposed, neither is it true that novelty could come about without the contribution of individuals, and that all individuals have the same likelihood of producing novelty. Luck, although a favorite explanationofcreativeindividuals explanation of creative individuals, is also easy to overstate. Many young scientists in Linus Pauling's generation were exposed to the arrival of quantum theory from Europe. Why didn't they see what this theory implied for chemistry, the way he saw it? Many women would have liked to become scientists in the 1940s. Why did so few take the opportunity when the doors to graduate training were opened to them? Being in the right place at the right time is clearly important. But many people never realize that they are standing in a propitious space/time convergence, andevenfewerknowwhattodo and even fewer know what to do when the realization hits them. INTERNALIZING THE SYSTEM A person who wants to make a creative contribution not only must work within a creative system but must also reproduce that system within his or her mind. In other words, the person must learn the rules and the content of the domain, as well as the criteria of selection, the preferences of the field. In science, it is practically impossible to make a creative contribution without internalizing the fundamentalknowledgeofthe fundamental knowledge of the domain. All scientists would agree with the words of Frank Offner, a scientist and inventor: "The important thing is that you must have a good, a very solid grounding in the physical sciences, before you can make any progress in understanding." The same conclusions are voiced in every other discipline. Artists agree that a painter cannot make a creative contribution without looking, and looking, and looking at previous art, and without knowing what other artists and critics consider good and bad art. Writers say that you havetoreadreadandreadsome have to read, read, and read some more, and know what the critics' criteria for good writing are, before you can write creatively yourself.*

An extremely lucid example of how the internalization of the system works is given by the inventor Jacob Rabinow. At first, he talks about the importance of what I have called the domain: So you need three things to be an original thinker. First, you have to have a tremendous amount of information—a big database if you like to be fancy. If you're a musicianyoushouldknowalot musician, you should know a lot about music, that is, you've heard music, you remember music, you could repeat a song if you have to. In other words, if you were born on a desert island and never heard music, you're not likely to be a Beethoven. You might, but it's not likely. You may imitate birds but you're not going to write the Fifth Symphony. So you're brought up in an atmosphere where you store a lot of information. So you have to have the kind of memory that you need for the kind of things you want to do. And you dothosethingswhichareeasy do those things which are easy and you don't do those things which are hard, so you get better and better by doing the things you do well, and eventually you become either a great tennis player or a good inventor or whatever, because you tend to do those things which you do well and the more you do, the easier it gets, and the easier it gets, the better you do it, and eventually you become very one-sided but you're very good at it and you're lousy at everything else because you don't do it well. This is what engineers call positive feedback. Sothesmalldifferencesatthe So the small differences at the beginning of life become enormous differences by the time you've done it for forty, fifty, eighty years as I've done it. So anyway, first you have to have the big database. Next Rabinow brings up what the person must contribute, which is mainly a question of motivation, or the enjoyment one feels when playing (or working?) with the contents of the domain: Then you have to be willing to pull the ideas, because you're interestedNowsomepeople interested.

Now, some people could do it, but they don't bother. They're interested in doing something else. So if you ask them, they'll, as a favor to you, say: "Yeah, I can think of something." But there are people like myself who like to do it. It's fun to come up with an idea, and if nobody wants it, I don't give a damn. It's just fun to come up with something strange and different. Finally he focuses on how important it is to reproduce in one's mind the criteria of judgment that the field uses: And then you must have the ability to get rid of the trash which you think of. You cannot think only of good ideas, or write only beautiful music. You must think of a lot of music, a lot of ideas, a lot of poetry, a lot of whatever. And if you're good, you must be able to throw out the junk immediately without even saying it. In other words, you get many ideas appearing and you discard them because you're well trained and you say, "that's junk." And when you see the good one, you say, "Oops, this sounds interestingLetmepursuethata interesting. Let me pursue that a little further." And you start developing it. Now, people don't like this explanation. They say, "What? You think of junk?" I say, "Yup. You must." You cannot a priori think only of good ideas. You cannot think only of great symphonies. Some people do it very rapidly. And this is a matter of training. And by the way, if you're not well trained, but you've got ideas, and you don't know if they're good or bad, then you send them to the Bureau of Standards, National Institute of Standards, where I work, and we evaluatethemAndwethrow evaluate them. And we throw them out. He was asked what constitutes "junk." Is it something that doesn't work, or— It doesn't work, or it's old, or you know that it will not gel. You suddenly realize it's not good. It's too complicated. It's not what mathematicians call "elegant." You know, it's not good poetry. And this is a matter of training. If you're well trained in technology, you see an idea and say, "Oh, God, this is terrible." First of all, it'stoocomplicatedSecondly it's too complicated. Secondly, it's been tried before. Thirdly, he could have done it in three different easier ways. In other words, you can evaluate the thing. That doesn't mean that he wasn't original. But he simply didn't do enough. If he were well trained, if he had the experience I had, and had good bosses and worked with great people, he could say this is not really a good idea. It's an idea, but it's not a good idea. And you have arguments with people. And you say, "Look, this is not a good way. Look at the number of parts you're gluing together. Look attheamountofenergyit'lltake at the amount of energy it'll take. This is really not good." And the guy says, "But to me it's new." I say, "Yup. To you it's new. It may be new to the world. But it's still not good." To say what is beautiful you have to take a sophisticated group of people, people who know that particular art and have seen a lot of it, and say this is good art, or this is good music, or this is a good invention. And that doesn't mean everybody can vote on it; they don't know enough. But if a group of engineers who work on newstufflookatitandsay new stuff look at it and say, "That's pretty nice," that's because they know. They know because they've been trained in it. And a good creative person is well trained. So he has first of all an enormous amount of knowledge in that field. Secondly, he tries to combine ideas, because he enjoys writing music or enjoys inventing. And finally, he has the judgment to say, "This is good, I'll pursue this further." It would be very difficult to improve on this description of how thesystemsmodelworksafteritis the systems model works after it is internalized. Drawing on over eighty years of varied experience, Rabinow has distilled with great insight what is involved in being a creative inventor. And as his words suggest, the same process holds for other domains, whether poetry, music, or physics.

2

Creative Personality

To be creative, a person has to internalize the entire system that makes creativity possible. So what sort of person is likely to do that? This question is very difficult to answer. Creative individuals are remarkable for their ability to adapt to almost any situation and to make do with whatever is at hand to reachtheirgoalsIfnothingelse reach their goals. If nothing else, this distinguishes them from the rest of us. But there does not seem to be a particular set of traits that a person must have in order to come up with a valuable novelty. What John Reed, the CEO of Citicorp, who has thought quite a lot about such things, says about businesspeople could be applied to creative persons in other domains as well: Well, because of my job, I tend to know the guys who run the top fifty, one hundred companies in the country, and there's quite a rangeIthaslittletodowiththe range. It has little to do with the industry. It's funny, there is a consistency in what people look at in businesspeople, but there's no consistency in style and approach, personality, and so forth. There is not a consistent norm with regard to anything other than business performance. Personality type, style. There are guys who drink too much, there are guys who chase girls; there are guys who are conservative, do none of the above; there are guys who are very serious and workaholics; therereguyswhoit'squite there are guys who—it's quite amazing, the range of styles. You're paid to run companies, they watch quite carefully as to results. But there's an amazing lack of consistency on any other dimension. How you do it seems to be a wide-open variable. There isn't a clear pattern, tremendously different personality types. And it doesn't seem to run by industry either. The same is true for scientists: What leads to an important discovery doesn't matter as long as you play by the rules. Or for artists: Youcanbeahappyextrovertlike You can be a happy extrovert like Raphael, or a surly introvert like Michelangelo—the only thing that matters is how good your *paintings are judged to be. This is all well and true; yet at the same time it is somewhat disappointing. After all, to say that what makes a person creative is his or her creativity is a tautology. Can we do any better? We don't really have very sound evidence, let alone proof, but we can venture some rather robust and credible suggestions. Perhaps the first trait that facilitates creativity is a genetic predispositionforagivendomain predisposition for a given domain. It makes sense that a person whose nervous system is more sensitive to color and light will have an advantage in becoming a painter, while someone born with a perfect pitch will do well in music. And being better at their respective domains, they will become more deeply interested in sounds and colors, will learn more about them, and thus are in a position to innovate in music or art with greater ease. On the other hand, a sensory advantage is certainly not necessaryElGrecoseemstohave necessary. El Greco seems to have suffered from a disease of the optic nerve, and Beethoven was functionally deaf when he composed some of his greatest work. Although most great scientists seem to have been attracted to numbers and experimentation early in life, how creative they eventually became bears little relationship to how talented they were as children. But a special sensory advantage may be responsible for developing an early interest in the domain, which is certainly an important ingredientofcreativityThe ingredient of creativity. The physicist John Wheeler remembers being interested in "toy mechanisms, things that would shoot rubber bands, Tinkertoys, toy railroads, electric light bulbs, switches, buzzers." His father, who was a librarian, used to take him to New York State University, where he left John in the library office while he lectured. John was fascinated by the typewriters and other machines, especially hand calculators: "You pushed a button down and turned a crank, and how the thing worked, that intrigued me immensely." When he was twelve, hebuiltaprimitivecalculatorthat he built a primitive calculator that had gears whittled out of wood. Without a good dose of curiosity, wonder, and interest in what things are like and in how they work, it is difficult to recognize an interesting problem. Openness to experience, a fluid attention that constantly processes events in the environment, is a great advantage for recognizing potential novelty. Every creative person is more than amply endowed with these traits. Here is how the historian Natalie Davis selects what historical projects to focus on: Well, I just get really curious about some problem. It just hooks in very deeply. At the time I don't know why necessarily it is that I invest so much curiosity and eros into some project. At the time, it just seems terribly interesting and important for the field. I may not know what is personally invested in it, other than my curiosity and my delight. Without such interest it is difficult to become involved in a domain deeply enough to reach its boundaries and then push them fartherTrueitispossibletomake farther. True, it is possible to make one creative discovery, even a very important one, by accident and without any great interest in the topic. But contributions that require a lifetime of struggle are impossible without curiosity and love for the subject. A person also needs access to a domain. This depends to a great extent on luck. Being born to an affluent family, or close to good schools, mentors, and coaches obviously is a great advantage. It does no good to be extremely intelligent and curious if I cannot learnwhatittakestooperateina learn what it takes to operate in a given symbolic system. The ownership of what sociologist Pierre Bourdieu calls "cultural capital" is a great resource. Those who have it provide their children with the advantage of an environment full of interesting books, stimulating conversation, expectations for educational advancement, role models, tutors, useful connections, and so on. But here too, luck is not everything. Some children fight their way to the right schools while their peers stay behind. Manfred EigenwascapturedbyRussian Eigen was captured by Russian troops at age seventeen and taken to a prisoner-of-war camp at the end of World War II, because he had been drafted to serve in an antiaircraft unit two years earlier. But he was determined to get back to studying science, even though he had had to leave high school at fifteen and never finished his studies. He escaped from the POW camp, walked back across half of Europe, and made a beeline for Göttingen, for he had heard that the best faculty in physics was reassembling there after the ravages of the war. He reached the city beforetheuniversityactuallyhada before the university actually had a chance to open but was admitted later with the first cohort of students, even though he lacked a high school diploma. Caught up in the ascetic postwar dedication to scholarship, led by the most knowledgeable teachers, surrounded by other equally dedicated students, he made quick progress. A few years later he received his doctorate and in 1967 the Nobel Prize. It is true that in early childhood Eigen could draw on substantial cultural capital, because his family had been musical and intellectually ambitiousNeverthelessfew ambitious. Nevertheless, few people tossed by fate so far outside the circle of knowledge found their way back to its center as quickly and surely as he did. Access to a field is equally important. Some people are terribly knowledgeable but are so unable to communicate with those who matter among their peers that they are ignored or shunned in the formative years of their careers. Michelangelo was reclusive, but in his youth was able to interact with leading members of the Medici court long enough to impress them with his skillanddedicationIsaacNewton skill and dedication. Isaac Newton was equally solitary and cantankerous, but somehow convinced his tutor at Cambridge that he deserved a lifetime tenured fellowship* at the university, and so was able to continue his work undisturbed by human contact for many years. Someone who is not known and appreciated by the relevant people has a very difficult time accomplishing something that will be seen as creative. Such a person may not have a chance to learn the latest information, may not be given the opportunity to work, and if he or she does manage to accomplishsomethingnovelthat accomplish something novel, that novelty is likely to be ignored or ridiculed. In the sciences, being at the right university—the one where the most state-of-the-art research is being done in the best equipped labs by the most visible scientists—is extremely important. George Stigler describes this as a snowballing process, where an outstanding scientist gets funded to do exciting research, attracts other faculty, then the best students—until a critical mass is formed that has an irresistible appeal to any young personenteringthefieldInthearts person entering the field. In the arts, the attraction is more to the centers of distribution, now primarily New York City, where the major galleries and collectors are located. Just as a century ago aspiring young artists felt they had to go to Paris if they wanted to be recognized, now they feel that unless they run the gauntlet of Manhattan they don't have a chance. One can paint beautiful pictures in Alabama or North Dakota, but they are likely to be misplaced, ignored, and forgotten unless they get the stamp of approval of critics, collectors, and other gatekeepers of the field. EvaZeisel'sworkreceivedthe Eva Zeisel's work received the imprimatur of the art establishment after her ceramics were shown by the Museum of Modern Art. The same is true of the other arts: Michael Snow spent ten years in New York City to catch up with the field of jazz music, and writers have to make connections with the agents and publishers there. Access to fields is usually severely restricted. There are many gates to pass, and bottlenecks form in front of them. Writers who want to catch the attention of an editor long enough to have their work read havetocompetewiththousandsof have to compete with thousands of similarly hopeful writers who have also submitted their manuscripts. The editor typically has only a few minutes to dedicate to each writer's work, assuming he or she even glances at the submission in the first place. Getting a literary agent to sell the manuscript is no solution either, since a good agent's attention is as difficult to get as that of an editor. Because of these bottlenecks, access to a field is often determined by chance or by irrelevant factors, such as having good connections. Studentsapplyingtogood Students applying to good universities in some disciplines are so many and have such excellent credentials that it is difficult to rank them in any meaningful way. Yet the openings are few, so a selection must be made. Hence the joke that the admissions committee throws all the application folders down a long stairway, *and the students whose files travel farthest get admitted. THE TEN DIMENSIONS OF COMPLEXITY Access to the domain and access to thefieldareallwellandgoodbut the field are all well and good, but when are we going to deal with the real characteristics of creative persons? When do we get to the interesting part—the tortured souls, the impossible dreams, the agony and the ecstasy of creation? The reason I hesitate to write about the deep personality of creative individuals is that I am not sure that there is much to write about, since creativity is the property of a complex system, and none of its components alone can explain it. The personality of an individual who is to do something creative must adapt itself to the particular domaintotheconditionsofa domain, to the conditions of a particular field, which vary at different times and from domain to domain. Giorgio Vasari in 1550 noted with chagrin that the new generations of Italian painters and sculptors seemed to be very different from their predecessors of the early Renaissance. They tended to be savage and mad, wrote the good Vasari, whereas their elders and betters had been tame and sensible. Perhaps Vasari was reacting to the artists who had embraced the ideology of Mannerism, the style usheredinbyMichelangelonearthe ushered in by Michelangelo near the end of his long career, which relied on interesting distortions of figures and on grand gestures. This style would have been considered ugly a hundred years earlier, and the painters who used it would have been shunned. But a few centuries later, at the height of the Romantic period, an artist who was not more than a little savage and mad would not have been taken very seriously, because these qualities were de rigueur for creative souls. In the 1960s, when abstract expressionism was the reigning stylethoseartstudentswhotended style, those art students who tended to be sullen, brooding, and antisocial were thought by their teachers to be very creative. They were encouraged, and they won the prizes and fellowships. Unfortunately, when these students left school and tried to establish careers in the art world, they found that being antisocial did not get them very far. To get the attention of dealers and critics they had to throw wild parties and be constantly seen and talked about. Hence a hecatomb of introverted artists ensued: Most were selected out, ending up as art teachers in the MidwestorascarsalesmeninNew Midwest or as car salesmen in New Jersey. Then the Warhol cohort replaced the abstract expressionists, and it was young artists with cool, clever, flip personalities who projected the aura of creativity. This, too, was a transient mask. The point is that you cannot assume the mantle of creativity just by assuming a certain personality style. One can be creative by living like a monk, or by burning the candle at both ends. Michelangelo was not greatly fond of women, while Picasso* couldn't get enough of them. Both changed the domain of painting, even though theirpersonalitieshadlittlein their personalities had little in common. Are there then no traits that distinguish creative people? If I had to express in one word what makes their personalities different from others, it would be complexity. By this I mean that they show tendencies of thought and action that in most people are segregated. They contain contradictory extremes— instead of being an "individual," each of them is a "multitude." Like the color white that includes all the hues in the spectrum, they tend to bring together the entire range of humanpossibilitieswithin human possibilities within themselves. These qualities are present in all of us, but usually we are trained to develop only one pole of the dialectic. We might grow up cultivating the aggressive, competitive side of our nature, and disdain or repress the nurturant, cooperative side. A creative individual is more likely to be both aggressive and cooperative, either at the same time or at different times, depending on the situation. Having a complex personality means being able to express the full rangeoftraitsthatarepotentially range of traits that are potentially present in the human repertoire but usually atrophy because we think that one or the other pole is "good," whereas the other extreme is "bad." This kind of person has many traits in common with what the Swiss analytic psychologist Carl Jung considered a mature personality. He also thought that every one of our strong points has a repressed shadow side that most of us refuse to acknowledge. The very orderly person may long to be spontaneous, the submissive person wishes to be dominant. As long as wedisowntheseshadowswecan we disown these shadows, we can never be whole or satisfied. Yet that is what we usually do, and so we keep on struggling against ourselves, trying to live up to an image that distorts our true being. A complex personality does not imply neutrality, or the average. It is not some position at the midpoint between two poles. It does not imply, for instance, being wishywashy, so that one is never very competitive or very cooperative. Rather it involves the ability to move from one extreme to the other as the occasion requires. Perhaps a centralpositionagoldenmeanis central position, a golden mean, is the place of choice, what software writers call the default condition. But creative persons definitely know both extremes and experience both with equal intensity and without inner conflict. It might be easier to illustrate this conclusion in terms of ten pairs of apparently antithetical traits that are often both present in such individuals and integrated with each other in a dialectical tension. 1. Creative individuals have a great deal of physical energy, but they are also often quiet and at restTheyworklonghourswith rest. They work long hours, with great concentration, while projecting an aura of freshness and enthusiasm. This *suggests a superior physical endowment, a genetic advantage. Yet it is surprising how often individuals who in their seventies and eighties exude energy and health remember a childhood plagued by illness. Heinz Maier-Leibnitz was bedridden for months in the Swiss mountains recovering from a lung ailment; György Faludy was often ill as a child, and so was the psychologist Donald Campbell. Public opinion analyst Elisabeth NoelleNeumannwasgivenno Noelle-Neumann was given no hope of survival by her physicians, but a homeopathic cure so improved her health that thirty years later she works harder than any four persons half her age. It seems that the energy of these people is internally generated and is due more to their focused minds than to the superiority of their genes. (Although it must be said that some respondents, such as Linus Pauling, answered "good genes," when asked to explain what accounted for their achievements.) This does not mean that creative personsarehyperactivealways persons are hyperactive, always "on," constantly churning away. In fact, they often take rests and sleep a lot. The important thing is that the energy is under their own control—it is not controlled by the calendar, the clock, an external schedule. When necessary they can focus it like a laser beam; when it is not, they immediately start recharging their batteries. They consider the rhythm of activity followed by idleness or reflection very important for the success of their work. And this is not a biorhythm they inherited with their genes; it waslearnedbytrialanderroras was learned by trial and error, as a strategy for achieving their goals. A humorous example is given by Robertson Davies: Well, you know, that leads me to something which I think has been very important in my life, and it sounds foolish and rather trivial. But I've always insisted on having a nap after lunch, and I inherited this from my father. And one time I said to him, "You know, you've done awfully well in the world. You came to Canada as an immigrant boy without anything and you havedoneverywellWhatdo have done very well. What do you attribute it to?" And he said, "Well, what drove me on to be my own boss was that the thing that I wanted most was to be able to have a nap every day after lunch." And I thought, What an extraordinary impulse to drive a man on! But it did, and he always had a twentyminute sleep after lunch. And I'm the same. I think it is very important. If you will not permit yourself to be driven and flogged through life, you'll probably enjoy it more. One manifestation of energy is sexualityCreativepeopleare sexuality. Creative people are paradoxical in this respect also. They seem to have quite a strong dose of eros, or generalized libidinal energy, which some express directly into sexuality. At the same time, a certain spartan celibacy is also a part of their makeup; continence tends to accompany superior achievement. Without eros, it would be difficult to take life on with vigor; without restraint, the energy could easily dissipate. 2. Creative individuals tend to be smart, yet also naive at the same timeHowsmarttheyactuallyare time. How smart they actually are is open to question. It is probably true that what psychologists call the g factor—meaning a core of general intelligence—is high among people who make important creative contributions. But we should not take seriously the lists that used to be printed on the sidebars of psychology textbooks, according to which John Stuart Mills must have had an IQ of 170 and Mozart an IQ of 135. Had they been tested at the time, perhaps they would have scored high. Perhaps not. And how many children in the eighteenthcenturywouldhave eighteenth century would have scored even higher but never did anything memorable? The earliest longitudinal study of superior mental abilities, initiated at Stanford University by the psychologist Lewis Terman in 1921, shows rather conclusively that children with very high IQs do well in life, but after a certain point IQ does not seem to be correlated any longer with superior performance in real life. Later studies suggest that the cutoff point is around 120; it might be difficult to do creative workwithalowerIQbutbeyond work with a lower IQ, but beyond 120 an increment in IQ does not necessarily imply higher creativity. Why a low intelligence interferes with creative accomplishment is quite obvious. But being intellectually brilliant can also be detrimental to creativity. Some people with high IQs get complacent, and, secure in their mental superiority, they lose the curiosity essential to achieving anything new. Learning facts, playing by the existing rules of domains, may come so easily toahighIQpersonthatheorshe to a high-IQ person that he or she never has any incentive to question, doubt, and improve on existing knowledge. This is probably why Goethe, among others, said that naïveté is the most important attribute of genius. Another way of expressing this dialectic is by the contrasting poles of wisdom and childishness. As Howard Gardner remarked in his study of the major creative geniuses of this century, a certain immaturity, both emotional and mental, can go hand in hand with deepest insights. Mozart comesimmediatelytomind comes immediately to mind. Furthermore, people who bring about an acceptable novelty in a domain seem able to use well two opposite ways of thinking: the convergent and the divergent. Convergent thinking is measured by IQ tests, and it involves solving well-defined, rational problems that have one correct answer. Divergent thinking leads to no agreed-upon solution. It involves fluency, or the ability to generate a great quantity of ideas; flexibility, or the ability to switch from one perspective to another; andoriginalityinpickingunusual and originality in picking unusual associations of ideas. These are the dimensions of thinking that most creativity tests measure and that most workshops try to enhance. It is probably true that in a system that is conducive to creativity, a person whose thinking is fluent, flexible, and original is more likely to come up with novel ideas. Therefore, it makes sense to cultivate divergent thinking in laboratories and corporations—especially if management is able to pick out andimplementthemost and implement the most appropriate ideas from the many that are generated. Yet there remains the nagging suspicion that at the highest levels of creative achievement the generation of novelty is not the main issue. A Galileo or a Darwin did not have that many new ideas, but the ones they fastened upon were so central that they changed the entire culture. Similarly, the individuals in our study often claimed to have had only two or three good ideas in their entire career, but each idea was so generative that it kept them busy foralifetimeoftestingfilling for a lifetime of testing, filling out, elaborating, and applying. Divergent thinking is not much use without the ability to tell a good idea from a bad one—and this selectivity involves convergent thinking. Manfred Eigen is one of several scientists who claim that the only difference between them and their less creative colleagues is that they can tell whether a problem is soluble or not, and this saves enormous amounts of time and many false starts. George Stigler stresses the importance of fluidity, thatisdivergentthinkingonthe that is, divergent thinking on the one hand, and good judgment in recognizing a viable problem on the other: I consider that I have good intuition and good judgment on what problems are worth pursuing and what lines of work are worth doing. I used to say (and I think this was bragging) that whereas most scholars have ideas which do not pan out more than, say, 4 percent of the time, mine come through maybe 80 percent of the time. 3. A third paradoxical trait refers totherelatedcombinationof to the related combination of playfulness and discipline, or responsibility and irresponsibility. There is no question that a playfully light attitude is typical of creative individuals. John Wheeler says that the most important thing in a young physicist is "this bounce, which I always associate with fun in science, kicking things around. It's not quite joking, but it has some of the lightness of joking. It's exploring ideas." David Riesman, in describing the attitude of "detached attachment" that makes him an astute observer ofthesocialscenestressesthe of the social scene, stresses the fact that he always "wanted at the same time to be irresponsible and responsible." But this playfulness doesn't go very far without its antithesis, a quality of doggedness, endurance, perseverance. Much hard work is necessary to bring a novel idea to completion and to surmount the obstacles a creative person inevitably encounters. When asked what enabled him to solve the physics problems that made him famous, Hans Bethe answered with a smile:*

"Two thingsarerequiredOneisa things are required. One is a brain. And second is the willingness to spend long times in thinking, with a definite possibility that you come out with nothing." Nina Holton, whose playfully wild germs of ideas are the genesis of her sculpture, is very firm about the importance of hard work: Tell anybody you're are a sculptor and they'll say, "Oh, how exciting, how wonderful." And I tend to say, "What's so wonderful?"Imeanit'slike wonderful?" I mean, it's like being a mason, or being a carpenter, half the time. But they don't wish to hear that because they really only imagine the first part, the exciting part. But, as Khrushchev once said, that doesn't fry pancakes, you see. That germ of an idea does not make a sculpture which stands up. It just sits there. So the next stage, of course, is the hard work. Can you really translate it into a piece of sculpture? Or will it be a wild thing which only seemed exciting while you were sitting in the studio alone? Willitlooklikesomething?Can Will it look like something? Can you actually do it physically? Can you, personally, do it physically? What do you have by way of materials? So the second part is a lot of hard work. And sculpture is that, you see. It is the combination of wonderful wild ideas and then a lot of hard work. Jacob Rabinow uses an interesting mental technique to slow himself down when work on an invention requires more endurance than intuition: Yeah, there's a trick I pull for thisWhenIhaveajobtodo this. When I have a job to do like that, where you have to do something that takes a lot of effort, slowly, I pretend I'm in jail. Don't laugh. And if I'm in jail, time is of no consequence. In other words, if it takes a week to cut this, it'll take a week. What else have I got to do? I'm going to be here for twenty years. See? This is a kind of mental trick. Because otherwise you say, "My God, it's not working," and then you make mistakes. But the other way, you say time is of absolutely no consequence. Peoplestartsayinghowmuch People start saying how much will it cost me in time? If I work with somebody else it's fifty bucks an hour, a hundred dollars an hour. Nonsense. You just forget everything except that it's got to be built. And I have no trouble doing this. I work fast, normally. But if something will take a day gluing and then next day I glue the other side—it'll take two days—it doesn't bother me at all. Despite the carefree air that many creative people affect, most of them work late into the night andpersistwhenlessdriven and persist when less driven individuals would not. Vasari wrote in 1550 that when the Renaissance painter Paolo Uccello was working out the laws of visual perspective, he would walk back and forth all night, muttering to himself: "What a beautiful thing is this perspective!" while his wife kept calling him back to bed with no success. Close to five hundred years later, physicist and inventor Frank Offner describes the time he was trying to understand how the membrane of *the ear works: Ah, the answer may come to meinthemiddleofthenight me in the middle of the night. My wife, when I was first into this membrane stuff, would kick me in the middle of the night and say, "Now get your mind off of membranes and get to sleep." 4. Creative individuals alternate between imagination and fantasy at one end, and a rooted sense of reality at the other. Both are needed to break away from the present without losing touch with the past. Albert Einstein once wrote that art and science are two of the greatest forms of escape from reality that humans have devisedInasensehewasright: devised. In a sense he was right: Great art and great science involve a leap of imagination into a world that is different from the present. The rest of society often views these new ideas as fantasies without relevance to current reality. And they are right. But the whole point of art and science is to go beyond what we now consider real, and create a new reality. At the same time, this "escape" is not into a never-never land. What makes a novel idea creative is that once we see it, sooner or later we recognize that, strange as it is, it is true. This dialectic is reflected by the way that, many years ago, the artists we studied responded to so-called projective tests, like the Rorschach or the Thematic Apperception Test. These require you to make up a story about some ambiguous stimuli, such as inkblots or drawings, that could represent almost anything. The more creative artists gave responses that were definitely more original, with unusual, colorful, detailed elements. But they never gave "bizarre" responses, which normal people occasionallydoAbizarre occasionally do. A bizarre response is one that, with all the goodwill in the world, one could not see in the stimulus. For instance if an inkblot looks vaguely like a butterfly, and you say that it looks like a submarine without being able to give a sensible clue as to what in the inkblot made you say so, the response would be scored as bizarre. Normal people are rarely original, but they are sometimes bizarre. Creative people, it seems, are original without being bizarre. The novelty they see is rooted in reality. Most of us assume that artists— musicians, writers, poets, painters —are strong on the fantasy side, whereas scientists, politicians, and businesspeople are realists. This may be true in terms of dayto-day routine activities. But when a person begins to work creatively, all bets are off—the artist may be as much a realist as the physicist, and the physicist as imaginative as the artist. We certainly think of bankers, for example, as having a rather pedestrian, commonsense view of whatisrealandwhatisnotYeta what is real and what is not. Yet a financial leader such as John Reed has much to say that dispels that notion. In his interview, he returns again and again to the theme that reality is relative and constantly changing, a perspective that he thinks is essential to confronting the future creatively: I don't think there is such a thing as reality. There are widely varying descriptions of reality, and you've got to be alert to when they change and what's really going on. No one is going to truly grasp it, but you havetostaytrulyactiveonthat have to stay truly active on that end. That implies you have to have a multifaceted perspective. There is a set of realities that exist at any moment in time. I always have some kind of a model in my mind as to what I think is going on in the world. I'm always tuning that [model] and trying to get different insights as I look at things, and I try to relate it back to what it means to our business, to how one behaves, if you will. I don't mean to say there isn't anythinginthecenterIjust anything in the center. I just think we can look at it [reality] in so many different ways. Right now, in my business, banks are deemed to be successful based on capital ratios. Ten years ago there was no concept of the "capital ratio." I failed totally to understand the impact of the savings and loan crisis on Congress, the regulators, and the industry. The world I'm living in today bears little resemblance to the world I lived in ten years ago, with regard to what was thought to be important. So we have defined a realitywhichasIsayisnot reality, which as I say is not empty, but it's close to being empty. Like anybody else, I was slow to recognize the new reality. Knowing these kinds of things turns out to be awfully relevant, because your degrees of freedom get taken away if you're off base. I went through a massive adjustment to play a game that was different from the one you saw before. But it's a changing reality. I know goddamn well that these capital ratios are not sufficiently robust tobelongtermdecentleading to be long-term, decent leading indicators of things, and five years from now the people who worry about how to price bank stocks are not going to be focusing on those. I describe success as evolutionary success. What Einstein implied about art and science reappears in this account of banking: It is an evolutionary process, where current reality becomes rapidly obsolete, and one must be on the alert for the shape of things to come. At the same time, the emergingrealityisnotafanciful emerging reality is not a fanciful conceit but something inherent in the here and now. It would be easy to dismiss Reed's visionary view as the romancing of a businessman who has had one too many encounters with reality. But apparently his unorthodox approach works: A recent issue of Newsweek announced: "John Reed might be excused a little gloating.... Since his darkest days three years ago he's quietly produced a stunning 425 percent return for investors who bought Citicorp shares." And one commentator adds that the overseasinvestmentsReedmade overseas investments Reed made were considered junk five years ago, whereas now they are seen as a hot stock. "Nothing's changed but the perception," the financial expert says, echoing Reed's take on the reality of the market. 5. Creative people seem to harbor* opposite tendencies on the continuum between extroversion and introversion. Usually each of us tends to be one or the other, either preferring to be in the thick of crowds or sitting on the sidelines and observing the passing show. In fact, in current psychologicalresearch psychological research, extroversion and introversion are considered the most stable personality traits that differentiate people from each other and that can be reliably measured. Creative individuals, on the other hand, seem to express both traits at the same time. The stereotype of the "solitary genius" is strong and gets ample support also from our interviews. After all, one must generally be alone in order to write, paint, or do experiments in a laboratory. As we know from studies of youngtalentedpeopleteenagers young talented people, teenagers who cannot stand being alone tend not to develop their skills because practicing music or studying math requires a solitude they dread. Only those teens who can tolerate being alone are able to master the symbolic content of a domain. Yet over and over again, the importance of seeing people, hearing people, exchanging ideas, and getting to know another person's work and mind are stressed by creative individuals. The physicist John Wheeler expresses this point with his usual directness:"Ifyoudon'tkick directness: "If you don't kick things around with people, you are out of it. Nobody, I always say, can be anybody without somebody being around." Physicist Freeman Dyson expresses with a fine nuance the opposite phases of this dichotomy in his work. He points to the door of his office and says: Science is a very gregarious business. It is essentially the difference between having this door open and having it shut. When I am doing science I have thedooropenImeanthatis the door open. I mean, that is kind of symbolic, but it is true. You want to be, all the time, talking with people. Up to a point you welcome being interrupted because it is only by interacting with other people that you get anything interesting done. It is essentially a communal enterprise. There are new things happening all the time, and you should keep abreast and keep yourself aware of what is going on. You must be constantly talking. But, of course, writing is different. When I am writing I have the doorshutandeventhentoo door shut, and even then too much sound comes through, so very often when I am writing I go and hide in the library. It is a solitary game. So, I suppose that is the main difference. But then, afterward, of course the feedback is very strong, and you get a tremendous enrichment of contacts as a result. Lots and lots of people write me letters simply because I have written books which address a general public, so I get into touch with a much wider circle of friends. It's broadened my horizons very much. But that is only after the writingisfinishedandnotwhile writing is finished and not while it is going on. John Reed builds the alternation between inner-directed reflection and intense social interaction into his daily routine: I'm an early morning guy. I get up at five always, get out of the shower about 5:30, and I typically try to work either at home or at the office, and that's when I do a good bit of my thinking and priority setting. I'm a great lister. I have twenty lists of things to do all the time. If I everhavefivefreeminutesIsit ever have five free minutes I sit and make lists of things that I should be worrying about or doing. Typically I get to the office about 6:30. I try to keep a reasonably quiet time until 9:30 or 10:00. Then you get involved in lots of transactions. If you are chairman of the company it's like being a tribal chieftain. People come into your office and talk to you. Even in the very private realm of the arts the ability to interact is essential. Nina Holton describes well the role of sociability in art: You really can't work entirely alone in your place. You want to have a fellow artist come and talk things over with you —"How does that strike you?" You have to have some sort of feedback. You can't be sitting there entirely by yourself and never show it. And then eventually, you know, when you begin to show, you have to have a whole network. You have to get to know gallery people, you have to get to know people who work in your field who are involved. And you may want to findoutwhetheryouwishtobe find out whether you wish to be part of it or not be part of it, but you cannot help being part of a fellowship, you know? Jacob Rabinow again puts into clear words the dilemma that many creative individuals face: I remember once we had a big party and Gladys [his wife] said that I sometimes walk to a different drummer. In other words, I'm so involved in an idea I'm working on, I get so carried away, that I'm all by myself. I'm not listening to what anybodysaysThissometimes anybody says. This sometimes happens. That you've got a new idea and you feel that it's very good and you're so involved that you're not paying attention to anybody. And you tend to drift away from people. It's very hard for me to be objective. I don't know. I'm social, I like people, I like to tell jokes, I like to go to the theater. But it's probably true that there are times when Gladys would have liked me to pay more attention to her and to the family. I love my children, they love me, and we have a wonderfulrelationshipButit wonderful relationship. But it could be that if I were not an inventor but had a routine job, I'd spend more time at home and I'd pay more attention to them, and the job would be something that I wouldn't like to do. So maybe people who don't like their jobs love their home more. It's quite possible. 6. Creative individuals are also remarkably humble and proud at the same time. It is remarkable to meet a famous person whom you expect to be arrogant or supercilious, only to encounter selfdeprecationandshyness self-deprecation and shyness instead. Yet there are good reasons why this should be so. In the first place, these individuals are well aware that they stand, in Newton's words, "on *the shoulders of giants." Their respect for the domain in which they work makes them aware of the long line of previous contributions to it, which puts their own into perspective. Second, they also are aware of the role that luck played in their own achievements. And third, they are usually so focused on future projects and current challengesthattheirpast challenges that their past accomplishments, no matter how outstanding, are no longer very interesting to them. Elisabeth Noelle-Neumann's answer to the question "Looking back on all your accomplishments, which one would you say you are most proud of?" is typical: I never think of what I am proud about. I never look back, except to find out about mistakes. Because mistakes are hard to remember and to draw conclusions from. But I only see danger in thinking back about thingsyouareproudofWhen things you are proud of. When people ask me if I am proud of something, I just shrug and hope to get away as soon as possible. I should explain that my way is always to look ahead, all my pleasant thoughts are about the future. It has been this way since I was twenty years old. I start every day fresh. The most important thing for me is to keep up the research institute, to keep up empirical research. Despite her great accomplishments and reputation in the field, neuropsychologist BrendaMilnertellsofbeingvery Brenda Milner tells of being very self-critical and of having enormous self-doubts about being creative. The Canadian artist Michael Snow attributes the restless experimentation that led him to so many successes to a sense of confusion and insecurity he has been trying to dispell. Another indication of modesty is how often this question was answered in terms of the family rather than the accomplishments that made a person famous. For instance, Freeman Dyson's answer was: "I suppose it is just tohaveraisedsixkidsand to have raised six kids, and brought them up, as far as one can see, all to be interesting people. I think that's what I am most proud of, really." And John Reed's: "Oh, God. That's real...I suppose being a parent. I have four kids. If you had to say what has both surprised and given you a lot of pleasure, I'd say that I'm close to my kids and I enjoy them, and I never would have guessed that that would be as much fun as it's turned out to be." At the same time, of course, no matter how modest these individualsaretheyknowthatin individuals are, they know that in comparison with others they have accomplished a great deal. And this knowledge provides a sense of security, even pride. This is often expressed as a sense of selfassurance. For instance, medical physicist Rosalyn Yalow mentioned repeatedly that all through her life she never had any doubts about succeeding in what she started out to do. Jacob Rabinow concurs: "There's one other thing that you do when you invent. And that is what I call the Existence Proof. This means that you have to assume that it can be doneIfyoudon'tassumethat done.*

If you don't assume that, you won't even try. And I always assume that not only it can be done, but I can do it." Some individuals stress humility, others self-assurance, but in actuality all of the people we interviewed seemed to have a good dose of both. Another way of expressing this duality is to see it as a contrast between ambition and selflessness, or competition and cooperation. It is often necessary for creative individuals to be ambitious and aggressive. Yet at thesametimetheyareoften the same time, they are often willing to subordinate their own personal comfort and advancement to the success of whatever project they are working on. Aggressiveness is required especially in fields where competition is acute, or in domains where it is difficult to introduce novelty. In George Stigler's words: Every scholar, I think, is aggressive in some sense. He has to be aggressive if he wants to change his discipline. Now, if you get a Keynes or a Friedman, theyarealsoaggressiveinthat they are also aggressive in that they want to change the world, and so they become splendid public figures as well. But that's a very hard game to play. Brenda Milner claims that the she has always been very aggressive verbally. John Gardner, statesman and founder of several national grassroots political organizations, describes well both the peaceful and aggressive instincts that coexist within the same person: I was the president of the CarnegieCorporationIhada Carnegie Corporation. I had a very interesting life, but not a lot of new challenges, not a tumultuous life. I was well protected. When I went to Washington I discovered a lot of things about myself that I didn't know. I discovered that I liked politicians. I got along well with them. I enjoyed dealing with the press, as much as anyone can enjoy dealing with the press. And then I discovered that I enjoyed a political fight, which was about as far away from my self-image as you can get. I'm a very peaceful person. ButthesethingscomeoutLife But these things come out. Life pulls them out of you, and as I say, I'm a slow learner, but in my midfifties I learned some interesting things. Several persons mention that in the course of their careers motivation has shifted from selfcentered goals to more altruistic interests. For instance, Sarah LeVine, who started out as an anthropologist and then became a fiction writer, has this to say: Up until quite recently, I used to think of production only for thegreatergloryofmyself the greater glory of myself, really. I don't see it that way at all anymore. I mean, it's nice if one gets recognition for what one does, but much more important is to leave something that other people can learn about, and I suppose that comes with middle age. 7. In all cultures, men are brought up to be "masculine" and to disregard and repress those aspects of their temperament that the culture regards as "feminine," whereas women are expected to do the opposite. Creative individualstoacertainextent individuals to a certain extent escape this rigid gender role stereotyping. When tests of masculinity/ femininity are given to young people, over and over one finds that creative and talented girls are more dominant and tough than other girls, and creative boys are more sensitive and less aggressive than their male peers. This tendency toward androgyny is sometimes understood in purely sexual terms, and therefore it gets confused with homosexuality. But psychological androgyny is a muchwiderconceptreferringto much wider concept, referring to a person's ability to be at the same time aggressive and nurturant, sensitive and rigid, dominant and submissive, regardless of gender. A psychologically androgynous person in effect doubles his or her repertoire of responses and can interact with the world in terms of a much richer and varied spectrum of opportunities. It is not surprising that creative individuals are more likely to have not only the strengths of their own gender but those of the other one, too. Among the people we interviewed, this form of androgyny was difficult to detect —no doubt in part because we did not use any standard test to measure its presence. Nevertheless, it was obvious that the women artists and scientists tended to be much more assertive, self-confident, and openly aggressive than women are generally brought up to be in our society. Perhaps the most noticeable evidence for the "femininity" of the men in the sample was their great preoccupationwiththeirfamily preoccupation with their family and their sensitivity to subtle aspects of the environment that other men are inclined to dismiss as unimportant. But despite having these traits that are not usual to their gender, they retained the usual gender-specific traits as well. In general, the women were perfectly "feminine" and the men thoroughly "masculine," in addition to having cross-gender traits. 8. Generally, creative people are thought to be rebellious and independent. Yet it is impossible tobecreativewithouthavingfirst to be creative without having first internalized a domain of culture. And a person must believe in the importance of such a domain in order to learn its rules; hence, he or she must be to a certain extent a traditionalist. So it is difficult to see how a person can be creative without being both traditional and conservative and at the same time rebellious and iconoclastic. Being only traditional leaves the domain unchanged; constantly taking chances without regard to what has been valued in the past rarely leads to novelty that is accepted as an improvement. The artistEvaZeiselwhosaysthat artist Eva Zeisel, who says that the folk tradition in which she works is "her home," nevertheless produces ceramics that were recognized by the Museum of Modern Art as masterpieces of contemporary design. This is what she says about innovation for its own sake: This idea to create something different is not my aim, and shouldn't be anybody's aim. Because, first of all, if you are a designer or a playful person in any of these crafts, you have to be able to function a long life, andyoucan'talwaystrytobe and you can't always try to be different. I mean different from different from different. Secondly, wanting to be different can't be the motive of your work. Besides—if I talk too much let me know—to be different is a negative motive, and no creative thought or created thing grows out of a negative impulse. A negative impulse is always frustrating. And to be different means not like this and not like that. And the "not like"—that's why postmodernism, with the prefix of "post" couldn't work. No negativeimpulsecanworkcan negative impulse can work, can produce any happy creation. Only a positive one. But the willingness to take risks, to break with the safety of tradition, is also necessary. The economist George Stigler is very emphatic in this regard: I'd say one of the most common failures of able people is a lack of nerve. They'll play safe games. They'll take whatever the literature's doing and add a little bit to it. In our field, for example, we study duopolywhichisasituationin duopoly, which is a situation in which there are two sellers. Then why not try three and see what that does. So there's a safe game to play. In innovation, you have to play a less safe game, if it's going to be interesting. It's not predictable that it'll go well. 9. Most creative persons are very passionate about their work, yet they can be extremely objective about it as well. The energy generated by this conflict between attachment and detachment has been mentioned by many as being animportantpartoftheirwork an important part of their work. Why this is the case is relatively clear. Without the passion, we soon lose interest in a difficult task. Yet without being objective about it, our work is not very good and lacks credibility. So the creative process tends to be what some respondents called a yinyang alternation between these two extremes. Here is how the historian Natalie Davis puts it: I am sometimes like a mother trying to bring the past to life again. I love what I am doing and I love to write. I just have a greatdealofaffectinvestedin great deal of affect invested in bringing these people to life again, in some way. It doesn't mean that I love my characters, necessarily, these people from the past. But I love to find out about them and re-create them or their situation. I think it is very important to find a way to be detached from what you write, so that you can't be so identified with your work that you can't accept criticism and response, and that is the danger of having as much affect as I do. But I am aware of that and of when I think it is particularly importanttodetachoneselffrom important to detach oneself from the work, and that is something where age really does help. 10. Finally, the openness and sensitivity of creative individuals often exposes them to suf ering and pain yet also a great deal of enjoyment. The suffering is *easy to understand. The greater sensitivity can cause slights and anxieties that are not usually felt by the rest of us. Most would agree with Rabinow's words: "Inventors have a low threshold of pain. Things bother them." A badly designed machine causes paintoaninventiveengineerjust pain to an inventive engineer, just as the creative writer is hurt when reading bad prose. Being alone at the forefront of a discipline also makes you exposed and vulnerable. Eminence invites criticism and often vicious attacks. When an artist has invested years in making a sculpture, or a scientist in developing a theory, it is devastating if nobody cares. Ever since the Romantic movement gained ascendance a few centuries ago, artists have been expected to suffer in order to demonstratethesensitivityof demonstrate the sensitivity of their souls. In fact, research shows that artists and writers do have unusually high rates of psychopathology and addictions. But what is the cause, what is the effect? The poet Mark Strand comments: There have been a lot of unfortunate cases of writers, painters, who have been melancholic, depressed, taken their own lives. I don't think it goes with the territory. I think those people would have been depressed, or alcoholic, suicidalwhatevereveniftkey suicidal, whatever, even if they weren't writing. I just think it's their characterological makeup. Whether that characterological makeup drove them to write or to paint, as well as to alcohol or to suicide, I don't know. I know there are an awful lot of healthy writers and painters who have no thoughts of suicide. I think it's a myth, by and large. It creates a special aura, a frailty, around the artist to say that he lives so close to the edge. He's so responsive to the world around him, so sensitive, so driven to respond to it, it's almostunbearableThathemust almost unbearable. That he must escape either through drugs or alcohol, finally suicide, the burden of consciousness is so great. But the burden of consciousness is great for people who don't—you know— want to kill themselves. It is also true that deep interest and involvement in obscure subjects often goes unrewarded, or even brings on ridicule. Divergent thinking is often perceived as deviant by the majority, and so the creative person may feel isolated and misunderstoodThese misunderstood. These occupational hazards do come with the territory, so to speak, and it is difficult to see how a person could be creative and at the same time insensitive to them. Perhaps the most difficult thing for a creative individual to bear is the sense of loss and emptiness experienced when, for some reason or another, he or she cannot work. This is especially painful when a person feels one's creativity drying out; then the whole self-concept is jeopardized, as Mark Strand suggests: suggests: Yeah, there's a momentary sereneness, a sense of satisfaction, when you come up with an idea that you think is worth pursuing. Another form of that is when you have completed, where you've done as much as you can with* an idea that you thought was worth working on. Then you sort of bask in the glow of completion for a day, maybe. You know, have a glass or two more of wine at night because you don't feel you have to go upstairs and lookatanythingagain look at anything again. And then you're beginning again. You hope. Sometimes the hiatus will last not overnight but for weeks, months, and years. And the longer the hiatus is between books that you're committed to finishing, the more painful and frustrating life becomes. When I say "painful," that's probably too grandiose a term for the petty frustration one feels. But if it goes on, and on, and you develop what people call a writer's block, it's painful, because your identity's atstakeIfyou'renotwriting at stake. If you're not writing, and you're a writer and known as a writer, what are you? Yet when the person is working in the area of his or her expertise, worries and cares fall away, replaced by a sense of bliss. Perhaps the most important quality, the one that is most consistently present in all creative individuals, is the ability to enjoy the process of creation for its own sake. Without this trait poets would give up striving for perfection and would write commercial jingles, economists wouldworkforbankswherethey would work for banks where they would earn at least twice as much as they do at the university, physicists would stop doing basic research and join industrial laboratories where the conditions are better and the expectations more predictable. In fact, enjoyment is such an important part of creativity that we devote chapter 5 to the connection. Here I report a single illustration, just as a place marker, to make sure that we don't lose sight of this essential component: Margaret Butler is a computer scientistandmathematicianthe scientist and mathematician, the first woman elected a fellow of the American Nuclear Society. In describing her work, like most of our respondents, she keeps stressing this element of fun, of enjoyment. In answer to the question "Of your accomplishments at work, what are you most proud of?" she answers: Well, in my work I think that the most interesting and exciting things that I have done were in the early days at Argonne when we were building computers. Weworkedonateamtodesign We worked on a team to design one of the first computers. We developed image analysis software with the people in the biology division for scanning chromosomes and trying to do automatic karyotyping, and I think that was the most fun that I had in all of my forty-plus years at the lab. It is interesting that this response, stressing fun and excitement, came in answer to a question about what she is most proud of in her work. Later on, she says: I worked and worked. You work hard. You try to do your best. When we were working on the chromosome project, Jim [her husband] and I spent sometimes the whole night over there working. We would come out in the morning and the sun would *be coming up. Science is very much fun. And I think women should have the opportunity to have fun. I may work as hard as Butler did out of ambition or a desire to make money. But unless I also enjoythetaskmymindisnot enjoy the task, my mind is not fully concentrated. My attention keeps shifting to the clock, to daydreams of better things to do, to resenting the job and wishing it was over. This kind of split attention, of halfhearted involvement, is incompatible with creativity. And creative people usually enjoy not only their work but also the many other activities in their lives. Margaret Butler, in describing what she does after her formal retirement, uses the word enjoy in reference to everything she does: helping her husband to continue his mathematical researchwritingacareersfor research, writing a careers-forwomen guide for the American Nuclear Society, working with teachers to get women students interested in science, organizing support groups for women scientists, reading, and being involved in local politics. These ten pairs of contrasting personality traits might be the most telling characteristic of creative people. Of course, this list is to a certain extent arbitrary. It could be argued that many other important traits have been left out. But what is important to keep in mindisthattheseconflictingtraits mind is that these conflicting traits —or any conflicting traits—are usually difficult to find in the same person. Yet without the second pole, new ideas will not be recognized. And without the first, they will not be developed to the point of acceptance. Therefore, the novelty that survives to change a domain is usually the work of someone who can operate at both ends of these polarities—and that is the kind of person we call "creative."*

3
Work In Creativity

Is there a single series of mental steps that leads to novelties that result in changing a domain? Or, to put it differently, is every creative product the result of a single "creative process"? Many individuals and business training programs claim that they know what "creative thinking" consists of and thattheycanteachitCreative that they can teach it. Creative individuals usually have their own theories—often quite different from one another. Robert Galvin says that creativity consists of anticipation and commitment. Anticipation involves having a vision of something that will become important in the future before anybody else has it; commitment is the belief that keeps one working to realize the vision despite doubt and discouragement. On the other hand, in his letter of refusal, the management guru Peter Drucker lists four reasons that accountforhisaccomplishments(in account for his accomplishments (in addition to the fifth, never participate in studies such as this): (a) I have been able to produce because I have always been a loner and have not had to spend time on keeping subordinates, assistants, secretaries, and other time-wasters; because (b) I never set foot in my university office—I do my teaching; and if students want to see me I give them lunch; because (c) I have been a workaholic since I was 20; and (d) because I thrive on stress and begin to pine if there is no deadlineOtherwiseifImaybe deadline. Otherwise—if I may be presumptuous: I was born like the sentry in Goethe's Faust II: Zum Sehen geboren Zum Schauen bestellt ("Born to see, my task is to watch") Given how different domains are from one another, however, and given the variety of tasks and the different strengths and weaknesses of individuals, we should not expect a great deal of similarity in how people arrive at a novel idea or product. Yet some common threadsdoseemtorunacross threads do seem to run across boundaries of domains and individual idiosyncrasies, and these might well constitute the core *characteristics of what it takes to approach a problem in a way likely to lead to an outcome the field will perceive as creative. Let's illustrate this process with a description of how the Italian author Grazia Livi wrote one of her short stories. THE WRITING OF A STORY One day Livi went to her bank to talk to a financial adviser who managed her portfolio of investmentsTheadviserwasa investments. The adviser was a woman Livi had met before; she seemed to her the epitome of a contemporary career woman bent on success and not much else, immaculately groomed, cold, hard, impatient. A person without a private life, with no dreams except money and advancement. This particular day the appointment started in the usual key: the adviser looking distant and frigid, asking questions in a dry, uninterested voice. Then a ringing phone interrupted the conversation. To Livi's surprise, as the woman turned away to take the call, her facechangedthechiseledfeatures face changed—the chiseled features softened, even the hard helmet of hair became velvety—her posture relaxed, her voice became low and caressing. Livi had an immediate visual image of the person at the other end of the phone: a handsome, tanned, laid-back architect who drove a Maserati. After returning from the bank, she made a few notes to herself in a log she keeps for this purpose and then apparently forgot the incident. Some months later, rereading the log, she saw a connection between the entry she had made of the episodeatthebankandentriesshe episode at the bank and entries she had written about a dressed-forsuccess woman sitting for hours in a beauty shop and other similar types she had met in the course of the past years. She was seized with a strong feeling of emotional discovery: Here was an insight about the current predicament of women— torn between contrasting demands —that could yield a true story. True not in the sense of representing what she had seen—the woman at the bank may have been talking to her mother or her child—but true to a widespread condition of our times, where many women feel that theyhavetobeaggressiveandcold they have to be aggressive and cold to compete in the business world yet at the same time cannot give up what they think of as their femininity. So she sat down to write about a career woman grooming herself all day for a date that never comes off—and it was a terrific story. Not because of the plot, which is as old as the hills, but because the emotional currents of her character reflected so achingly and accurately the experience of our time. Livi's story may not change the domain of literature, and hence it is notanexampleofthehighestorder not an example of the highest order of creativity. But it may well be included in future collections of short stories, because it is an excellent example of a contemporary genre. And to the extent that it expands the domain, it qualifies as a creative achievement. Is there a way to analyze what Livi* did, to see more clearly what her mental processes were as she wrote the story? The creative process has traditionally been described as taking five steps. The first is a period of preparation, becoming immersedconsciouslyornotina immersed, consciously or not, in a set of problematic issues that are interesting and arouse curiosity. In the case of Grazia Livi, the emotional quandary of modern women was something she experienced personally, as a writer trying to compete for prizes, reviews, and publications, and also as a woman trying to balance the responsibilities of motherhood with her writing. The second phase of the creative process is a period of incubation, during which ideas churn around below the threshold of consciousnessItisduringthistime consciousness. It is during this time that unusual connections are likely to be made. When we intend to solve a problem consciously, we process information in a linear, logical fashion. But when ideas call to each other on their own, without our leading them down a straight and narrow path, unexpected combinations may come into being. The third component of the creative process is insight, sometimes called the "Aha!" moment, the instant when Archimedes cried out "Eureka!" as he stepped into the bath, when the piecesofthepuzzlefalltogetherIn pieces of the puzzle fall together. In real life, there may be several insights interspersed with periods of incubation, evaluation, and elaboration. For instance, in the case of Livi's short story, there are at least two moments of significant insight: when she saw the investment adviser transformed by the phone call, and when she saw the connection between the similar entries in the log. The fourth component is evaluation, when the person must decide whether the insight is valuable and worth pursuing. This isoftenthemostemotionallytrying is often the most emotionally trying part of the process, when one feels most uncertain and insecure. This is also when the internalized criteria of the domain, and the internalized opinion of the field, usually become prominent. Is this idea really novel, or is it obvious? What will my colleagues think of it? It is the period of self-criticism, of soulsearching. For Grazia Livi, much of this sifting took place as she read through her log and decided which ideas to develop. The fifth and last component of the process is elaboration. It is probablytheonethattakesupthe probably the one that takes up the most time and involves the hardest work. This is what Edison was referring to when he said that creativity consists of 1 percent inspiration and 99 percent perspiration. In Livi's case, elaboration consisted in selecting the characters of the story, deciding on a plot, and then translating the emotions she had intuited into strings of words. But this classical analytic framework leading from preparation to elaboration gives a severely distorted picture of the creativeprocessifitistakentoo creative process if it is taken too literally. A person who makes a creative contribution never just slogs *through the long last stage of elaboration. This part of the process is constantly interrupted by periods of incubation and is punctuated by small epiphanies. Many fresh insights emerge as one is presumably just putting finishing touches on the initial insight. As Grazia Livi was struggling to find words to describe her character, the words themselves suggested new emotions that were sometimes more "right" to the personality she was trying to create than the ones she hadinitiallyenvisionedThesenew had initially envisioned. These new feelings in turn suggested actions, turns of the plot she had not thought of before. The character became more complex, more nuanced, as the writing progressed; the plot became more subtle and intriguing. Thus the creative process is less linear than recursive. How many iterations it goes through, how many loops are involved, how many insights are needed, depends on the depth and breadth of the issues dealt with. Sometimes incubation lasts for years; sometimes it takes a few hours. Sometimes the creative ideaincludesonedeepinsightand idea includes one deep insight and innumerable small ones. In some cases, as with Darwin's formulation of the theory of evolution, the basic insight may appear slowly, in separate disconnected flashes that take years to coalesce into a coherent idea. By the time Darwin clearly understood what his theory implied, it was hardly an insight any longer, because its components had all emerged in his thought at different times in the past and had slowly connected with one another along the way. It was a thunderous "Aha!" built up over a lifetime, made up of a chorus of little "Eurekas" "Eurekas." A more linear account is Freeman Dyson's description of the creative process that brought him scientific fame. Dyson had been a student of Richard Feynman, who in the late 1940s was trying to make electrodynamics understandable in terms of the principles of quantum mechanics. Success in this task would mean translating the laws of electricity so that they conformed to the more basic laws of subatomic behavior. It would be a great simplification, a welcome ordering of the domain of physics. Unfortunatelywhilemost Unfortunately, while most colleagues felt that Feynman was onto something deep and important, not many could follow the few scribbles and sketches he used to prove his points, especially since he usually went from A directly to Z with no stops in between. At the same time, another physicist, Julian Schwinger, also was working on the unification of quantum and electrodynamic principles. Schwinger was in many ways Feynman's opposite: He worked slowly and methodically and was such a perfectionist that he never felt ready to claim a solution to the problemhewasworkingon problem he was working on. Freeman Dyson, working in Feynman's orbit at Cornell University, was exposed to a series of lectures by Schwinger. It gave him the idea of bringing together Feynman's leaps of intuition with Schwinger's painstaking calculations and to resolve once and for all the puzzle of how the behavior of quanta related to electrical phenomena. After Dyson finished his work, Feynman's and Schwinger's theories became understandable, and the two received the Nobel Prize in physics. Several colleagues felt that ifanyonedeservedtheprizeitwas if anyone deserved the prize, it was Dyson. Here is how he describes the process that led to his accomplishment: It was the summer of 1948, so I was then twenty-four. There was a big problem which essentially the whole community of physicists was concentrated on. Physics is usually like that—there is some particularly fascinating problem that everybody is working on and it tends to be sort of one thing at a time. And at that time the big problem was called quantum electrodynamics, which wasatheoryofradiationand was a theory of radiation and atoms, and the theory was in a mess and nobody knew how to calculate with it. It was sort of a logjam for all kinds of further developments. So somebody had to learn how to calculate with this theory. It wasn't a question of the theory being wrong, but it was somehow not decently organized, so that people tried to calculate and always got silly answers, like zero or infinity, or something. Anyhow, at that moment there appeared two great ideas which were associated with two people, Schwinger and Feynman, both of themaboutfiveyearsolderthanI them about five years older than I was. Each of them produced a new theory of radiation, which looked as though it was going to work, although there were difficulties with both of them. I was in this happy position of being familiar with both of them and I got to know both of them and I got to work. I spent six months working very hard to understand both of them clearly, and that meant simply hard, hard work of calculating. I would sit down for days and days with large stacks of papers doing calculationssothatIcould calculations so that I could understand precisely what Feynman was saying. And at the end of six months, I went off on a vacation. I took a Greyhound bus to California and spent a couple of weeks just bumming around. This was soon after I had arrived from England, so I had never been to the West before. After two weeks in California, where I wasn't doing any work, I was just sight-seeing, I got on the bus to come back to Princeton, and suddenly in the middle of the night when we were going through Kansas, the whole sort of suddenlybecamecrystalclear suddenly became crystal clear, and so that was sort of the big revelation for me, it was the Eureka experience or whatever you call it. Suddenly the whole picture became clear, and Schwinger fit into it beautifully and Feynman fit into it beautifully and the result was a theory that actually was useful. That was the big creative moment of my life. Then I had to spend another six months working out the details and writing it all up and so forth. It finally ended up with two long papers in the Physical Review, and that was my passport to the worldofscience world of science. It would be difficult to imagine a clearer example of the classical version of the creative process. It starts with Dyson, immersed in the field of physics, sensing from his teachers and colleagues where the next opportunity for adding something important to the domain lies. He has a privileged access to both the domain and the field—he is personally acquainted with the two central individuals involved. Having found his problem—to reconcile the two leading theories in the domain—he goes through a sixmonthperiodofconsciously six-month period of consciously directed, hard preparation. Then he spends two weeks relaxing, a period during which the ideas marshaled up during the past half year have a chance to incubate, to sort out and shake together. This is followed by the sudden insight that occurs unbidden during a night bus ride. And finally another half year of hard work evaluating and elaborating the insight. The idea having been accepted by the field— in this case, the editors of Physical Review—it is then added to the domain. As is often the case, most of the credit for the accomplishment doesnotgodirectlytotheauthor does not go directly to the author, but to those whose work he has built upon. The five-stage view of the creative process may be too simplified, and it can be misleading, but it does offer a relatively valid and simple way to organize the complexities involved. Therefore, I use these categories to describe how creative people work, starting with the beginning phase, that of preparation. It is essential to remember in what follows, however, that the five stages in reality are not exclusive buttypicallyoverlapandrecur but typically overlap and recur several times before the process is completed. THE EMERGENCE OF PROBLEMS Occasionally it is possible to arrive at a creative discovery without any preparation. The fortunate person simply stumbles into a wholly unpredictable situation, as Roentgen did when he tried to find out why his photographic plates were being ruined and discovered radiation in the process. But usually insights tend to come to prepared minds, thatistothosewhohavethought that is, to those who have thought long and hard about a given set of problematic issues. There are three main sources from which problems typically arise: personal experiences, requirements of the domain, and social pressures. While these three sources of inspiration are usually synergistic and intertwined, it is easier to consider them separately, as if they acted independently, which in reality is not the case. Life as a Source of Problems We have seen that Grazia Livi's ideaforastoryabouttheconflict idea for a story about the conflict between career and femininity was influenced by her own experiences as a woman. From the time she was a little girl, her parents expected* her two brothers to be educated and successful while Grazia and her sister were expected to grow up to be traditional housewives. Throughout her life Livi rebelled against the role cut out for her. Even though she married and had children, she resolved to become successful on her own. It is this direct experience in her own life that made her sensitive to the episodes involving career women thatshejotteddowninherdiary that she jotted down in her diary. The origins of problematic elements in life experience are easiest to see in the work of artists, poets, and humanists in general. Eva Zeisel, who was considered the "dumb one" in a family that eventually included two Nobel laureates and many other outstanding male scientists, also resolved to prove herself by breaking away from traditional family interests and becoming an independent artist. Most of the creative ideas for her pottery come from a tension between two contrastingselfimposed contrasting, self-imposed requirements: to make pots that conform to the human hand and are steeped in tradition, and yet can be mass-produced inexpensively by modern technology. Poets like Anthony Hecht, György Faludy, and Hilde Domin write down daily impressions, events, and especially feelings on index cards or in notebooks, and these caches of experience are the raw material out of which their work evolves. "I had a friend, a poet called Radnòty, who wrote poems I considered atrocious," says Faludy. "Andthenaftersufferinginthe "And then after suffering in the concentration camps it changed him totally and he wrote wonderful verse. Suffering is not bad: It helps you very much. Do you know a novel about happiness? Or a film about happy people? We are a perverse race, only suffering interests us." He then relates how once when he was sitting in a cabin on beautiful Vancouver Island, trying to find inspiration to start a poem, he could think of nothing interesting. Finally, a set of strong images occurred to him: Five secret policemen arrive in a boat, break into the cabin, throw his books out ofthewindowintotheseatakehim of the window into the sea, take him five thousand miles to Siberia, and beat him mercilessly—a great scenario for a poem, one with which the poet was unfortunately all too familiar. The historian Natalie Davis describes the project she is working on, a book about three women of the seventeenth century, one Jewish, one Catholic, one Protestant, exploring the "sources of adventuresomeness for women": They were all sort of me in the sense that they were all middleagedmothersalthoughinone aged mothers, although in one case a grandmother—which I am —and so I keep thinking that it is no coincidence that I got started on this completely different project. The painter Ed Paschke tears off dozens of arresting images each day from magazines and newspapers and keeps these strange or funny cutouts in boxes to which he returns occasionally for inspiration. Rummaging through these *icons of the times he may find one that he projects on the wall and uses as a starting point for a sardonic pictorialcommentaryAnother pictorial commentary. Another painter, Lee Nading, tears off newspaper headlines that have to do with the conflict of nature and technology—DAM ENDANGERS RARE FISH or TRAIN FULL OF GARBAGE DERAILS IN IOWA— and eventually uses one of them to inspire a canvas. To understand why Nading is particularly sensitive to this kind of event, it helps to know that he had a beloved elder brother who committed suicide just as his career was becoming successful. This brother worked at one of the most prestigious scientific research laboratoriesbutbecame laboratories but became disillusioned with the competitiveness and the lack of concern for human consequences that he felt around him. Nading never quite forgave science for having contributed to his brother's death, and he finds in the threats posed by the fruits of science the source for his artistic problems. Artists find inspiration in "real" life—emotions like love and anxiety, events like birth and death, the horrors of war, and a peaceful afternoon in the country. We shall see in a little while that artists are alsoinfluencedinthechoiceof also influenced in the choice of their problems by the domain and the field. It has been said that every painting is a response to all previous paintings, and every poem reflects the history of poetry. Yet paintings and poems are also very clearly inspired by the artist's experiences. The experiences of scientists are relevant to the problems they deal with in a much more general, but perhaps not less important way. This has to do with the fundamental interest and curiosity the scientist brings to the task. One of the very firststudiesofcreativescientists first studies of creative scientists, conducted by Ann Roe, concluded that the chemists and physicists in her sample became interested as children in the properties of matter because the normal interests of childhood were not accessible to them. Their parents were emotionally distant, they had few friends, they were not very athletic. Perhaps this kind of generalization is drawn with too thick a brush, but the basic idea underlying it—that early experience predisposes a young person to be interested in a certain range of problems—is probably sound. For instance, the physicist Viktor Weisskopf, describes with great emotion the sense of awe and wonder he felt when, as a young man, he and a friend used to climb in the Austrian Alps. Many of the great physicists of his generation, like Max Planck, Werner Heisenberg, and Hans Bethe, claim that what inspired them to try to understand the movement of atoms and stars was the exhilaration they felt at the sight of tall peaks and the night sky. Linus Pauling became interested inchemistrywhenhisfathera in chemistry when his father, a pharmacist in turn-of-the-century Portland, let him mix powders and potions in the back of the drugstore. The young Pauling was fascinated by the fact that two* different substances could turn into a third entirely different one. He experienced a godlike sense of being able to create something entirely new. By the age of seven he had read and practically memorized the enormous Pharmacopoeia containing the knowledge of basic elements and mixtures a pharmacist was expected to know. It was this early curiosity about how matter couldbetransformedthatfueled could be transformed that fueled Pauling's career for the next eighty years. The psychologist Donald Campbell makes the point that the difference between a scholar who comes up with new ideas and one who does not is often a difference in curiosity: So many of my professor friends who know that they should be continuing to do research look around and find no problem that fascinates them. Whereas I have a scattered dilettante backlog of problems that I would love to work on and I feel are within reachofasolutionManytalented reach of a solution. Many talented people can't think of anything to do that they feel is worth doing. Now, I think that I am blessed that there are trivial problems that can excite me. Without a burning curiosity, a lively interest, we are unlikely to persevere long to make a significant new contribution. This kind of interest is rarely only intellectual in nature. It is usually rooted in deep feelings, in memorable experiences that need some sort of resolution—a resolution that can be achieved only by a new artistic expression or a newwayofunderstanding new way of understanding. Someone who is motivated solely by the desire to become rich and famous might struggle hard to get ahead but will rarely have enough inducement to work beyond what is necessary, to venture beyond what is already known. The Influence of Past Knowledge The other main source of problems is the domain itself. Just as personal experiences produce tensions that cannot be resolved in terms of ordinary solutions, so does working within a symbolic system. Over and overbothintheartsandthe over, both in the arts and the sciences, the inspiration for a creative solution comes from a conflict suggested by the "state of the art." Every domain has its own internal logic, its pattern of development, and those who work within it must respond to this logic. A young painter in the 1960s had two choices: Either paint in the fashionable abstract expressionist style or discover a viable way of rebelling against it. Natural scientists in the early part of this century were confronted by the development of quantum theory in physics: Many of the most challengingproblemsinchemistry challenging problems in chemistry, biology, astronomy, as well as physics, were generated by the possibility of applying quantum theory to these new realms. Freeman Dyson's concern with quantum electrodynamics is only one example. Gerald Holton, a physicist who later turned to the history of science, gives a lucid account of how a problematic issue in the domain can fuse with a personally felt conflict to suggest the theme *for a person's lifework. As a graduate student at Harvard, Holton was immersedintheheadyatmosphere immersed in the heady atmosphere of logical positivism. His teachers and fellow students were bent on demonstrating that science could be reduced to an absolutely logical enterprise. Nothing intuitive or metaphysical was admitted to this new domain. But Holton, who read about the way Kepler and Einstein had worked, started to feel that the kind of science everyone around him took for granted did not apply to some of the most celebrated scientific breakthroughs. I discovered that these models don't quite work, that you do not infacthavebuiltintousual in fact have built into usual accounts of the scientific process the kind of presuppositions that these people were very fond of. It was not true, for example, that the way to think about science is to think in terms of protocol sentences, and verification theory of meaning, and all of those things that were very dear to them. But these presuppositions were the things that the best of them were willing to put their money on, their reputation, their time, their very life, and stick with it even against the evidence for a while. They were enchanted with an idea forwhichtherewasinfactno for which there was in fact no proof. I had to really struggle with that. And it is at that point that I found the idea of a thematic proposition, that some people are imbued with prior thematic ideas which would survive a period of disconfirmation. And that was not part of the logic of positivism or empiricism at all. Holton describes the genesis of his own intellectual problem as a conjunction of personal interest and a sense that something was askew intheintellectualenvironment: in the intellectual environment: Your research project gets defined partly by some internal fascination for which one cannot account in any detail, preparation that is unique because of the life history of that person, luck, and something to work against. That is, something that you are dissatisfied with that other people are doing. An intellectual problem is not restricted to a particular domain. Indeed, some of the most creative breakthroughs occur when an idea thatworkswellinonedomaingets that works well in one domain gets grafted to another and revitalizes it. This was certainly the case with the widespread applications of physics' quantum theory to neighboring disciplines like chemistry and astronomy. Creative people are ever alert to what colleagues across the fence are doing. Manfred Eigen, whose recent work involves the attempt to replicate inorganic evolution in the laboratory, is bringing together concepts and experimental procedures from physics, chemistry, and biology. The ideas coalesced in part from conversations over the years with colleaguesfromdifferent colleagues from different disciplines—whom he invited to informal winter meetings in Switzerland. A large majority of our respondents were inspired by a tension in their domain that became obvious when looked at from the perspective of another domain. Even though they do not think of themselves as interdisciplinary, their best work bridges realms of ideas. Their histories tend to cast doubt on the wisdom of overspecialization, where bright young people are trained to become exclusiveexpertsinonefieldand exclusive experts in one field and shun breadth like the plague. And then there are people who sense problems in "real" life that cannot be accommodated within the symbolic system of any existing domain. Barry Commoner, trained as a biophysicist, decided to step out of the formalities of the academic approach and confront such issues as the quality of water and the disposal of garbage. His problems are defined by real-life concerns, not disciplines. Well, I established a pretty good reputationinbiochemistryand reputation in biochemistry and biophysics. In the beginning all of the papers were published in academic journals. But in various ways and for various reasons I moved more and more in the direction of doing work that was relevant to real world problems. And every now and then a paper of mine will appear in an academic journal, but that's just by accident. As the generation of World War II scientists began to get older, the academic world became very isolated from the real world. Academicworkwasdiscipline Academic work was discipline dictated and discipline oriented, which is really pretty dull, I think. The prevailing philosophy in academic life is reductionism, which is exactly the reverse of my approach to things, and I'm not interested in doing it. This is a typical reaction against a domain becoming too confining and its members mistaking the symbolic system in which they operate for the broader reality of which it is a part. Commoner's feelings may be similar to those that young scholars inByzantiummusthavefeltwhen in Byzantium must have felt when the church councils spent so much time debating how many angels could dance on the head of a pin. When a field becomes too selfreferential and cut off from reality, it runs the risk of becoming irrelevant. It is often dissatisfaction with the rigidity of domains that makes great creative advances possible. Of course, a person cannot be inspired by a domain unless he or she learns its rules. That is why everyone we talked to, whether artist or scientist, emphasized over andovertheimportanceofbasic and over the importance of basic knowledge, of thorough familiarity with the symbolic information and the basic procedures of the discipline. György Faludy can recite long stretches of verse by Catullus that he memorized in Latin sixty years ago; he has read all the Greek, Chinese, Arabic, and European poetry that he has been able to find. He translated more than fourteen hundred poems from around the world to master his craft, even though his own powerful poems are simple, discursive, and based on personal experience.*

In science, mastery of the basic symbolictoolsisequallyimportant symbolic tools is equally important. Practically everyone echoes what Margaret Butler tells high school students: The message that we were trying to get [across] is that if you do not know what you want to be, at least take science and math. Especially math, so that when you get into college if you change your mind and you like science or math more, or you find that you want to get into it, then you will have the background that is needed. Many women find later on that they do not have the background [mathematics]becausethey [mathematics] because they copped out early on. You cannot transform a domain unless you first thoroughly understand how it works. Which means that one has to acquire the tools of mathematics, learn the basic principles of physics, and become aware of the current state of knowledge. But the old Italian saying seems to apply: Impara l'arte, e mettila da parte (learn the craft, and then set it aside). One cannot be creative without learning what others know, but then one cannot be creative without becomingdissatisfiedwiththat becoming dissatisfied with that knowledge and rejecting it (or some of it) for a better way. The Pressures of the Human Environment The third source of ideas and problems is the field one works in. All through life, a creative person is exposed to the influence of teachers, mentors, fellow students, and coworkers, and later in life to the ideas of one's own students and followers. Moreover, the institutions one works for and the events of the wider society in which onelivesprovidepowerful one lives provide powerful influences that can redirect one's career and channel a person's thinking in new directions. Indeed, if we look at creativity from this perspective, personal experience and domain knowledge may pale in comparison with the contribution of the social context to determine which problems one tackles. What an artist paints is a response not only to the classic canon of art but also to what others are painting right now. Scientists don't learn only from books or experiments they conduct but also fromseminarsmeetings from seminars, meetings, workshops, and journal articles reporting what is happening, or about to happen elsewhere. Whether one follows the crowd or takes a different path, it is usually impossible to ignore what takes place in the field. Many people are introduced to the wonders of a domain by a teacher. There is often a particular teacher who recognizes the child's curiosity or ability and starts cultivating his or her mind in the discipline. Some creative persons have a long list of such teachers. The critic and rhetoricianWayneBoothsaysthat rhetorician Wayne Booth says that each year in school he idealized a different one and tried to live up to that teacher's expectations. In his case, as in several others, the changes from one career direction to the other—from engineering to English—occurred in response to the quality of the teachers encountered. For some, the introduction to the domain comes later. John Gardner started college intending to become a writer but found in the psychology departments of Berkeley and then Stanford an intellectual community thatsatisfiedhiscuriosityaswell that satisfied his curiosity as well as his desire for congenial company. The field is paramount for individuals who work primarily in an organizational context. John Reed of Citicorp must constantly interact with several groups in order to assimilate the information that he needs to make difficult decisions. About twice a year he meets for a few days with the halfdozen heads of the national banks of Germany, Japan, and so on to exchange ideas about future trends in the world economy. At more frequentintervalshehassimilar frequent intervals he has similar meetings with the CEOs of General Motors, General Electric, or IBM. Even more often, he meets with the key executives of his own corporation. His inner network consists of about thirty people whom he trusts to provide the input he needs to navigate a multibilliondollar corporation through constantly changing times. Reed spends at least half of his mornings talking on the phone or in person with members of this network and never makes a major decision involving the company without conferring with at least some of them them. Another organizational approach is represented by Robert Galvin, president of Motorola. Galvin sees his company as a gigantic creative enterprise, with more than twenty thousand engineers anticipating trends, reacting to them with new ideas, creating new products and processes. He sees his own job as orchestrating all this effort, being a role model for everyone else. In cases when the responsibility is to lead a group of people in novel directions, work is usually dictated not by a symbolic domain but by the requirementsoftheorganization requirements of the organization itself. It could be said for them, to borrow Marshall McLuhan's phrase, that the medium is the message; what they accomplish within their organizational structure is their creative accomplishment. Scientists also mention the importance of particular research institutions. The Bell Labs, the Rockefeller Institute, and the Argonne National Laboratories are some of the places that have allowed young scientists to pursue their interests in a stimulating and supportive environment. Not surprisinglymanyofthemfeel surprisingly, many of them feel strong loyalties to such institutions and are more than willing to follow their research policies. Many a Nobel Prize was won by tackling problems that arose out of such institutional contexts. New ideas are also generated when someone attempts to create a new organization or perhaps a new field. Manfred Eigen founded an interdisciplinary Max Planck Institute in Göttingen to replicate experimentally evolutionary forces in the laboratory. George Klein built up the tumor biology research center at the Karolinska Institute in center at the Karolinska Institute in Stockholm, and employs a large cadre of Ph.D.'s. Initiatives of this sort not only allow the principal investigator to pursue his or her research but also make it possible for a new discipline to emerge. If the lab is successful, entirely new sets of problems are opened up for investigation, and with time a new symbolic system—or domain—may develop. Finally, some creative individuals attempt to form entirely new organizations outside the pale of accepted scientific, academic, or business institutions Hazel business institutions. Hazel Henderson dedicates most of her time to developing groups that will further her vision; she sees herself as the progenitor of innumerable special interest groups united in their ecological consciousness. Similarly, Barry Commoner has purposefully positioned his center in a no-man's-land where he can move unfettered by the pressures of academic or political conformity. When John Gardner founded Common Cause, he insisted on financing it only through small independent contributions so as to avoid the major influences that come with large donations By come with large donations. By creating new forms of association, these individuals hope to see new problems emerge, leading to solutions that couldn't be attempted through old ways of thinking. But organizations are embedded in larger human groups and broader historical processes. An economic depression or a change in political priorities will stimulate one line of research and send another into oblivion. According to George Stigler, the Great Depression is what sent him and many of his colleagues to study economics in graduate school The availability of graduate school. The availability of nuclear reactors built to support World War II projects stimulated many bright students to major in physics. György Faludy spent many years in concentration camps for writing one poem critical of Joseph Stalin. Wars are notorious for affecting the direction of science, and, indirectly, of the arts as well. Let's take psychology as an example. The domain of mental testing, including the whole concept of the IQ test and its uses, owes much of its success to the U.S. Army's need to have a way of selecting recruits for World way of selecting recruits for World War I. Afterward the testing technology was transported into the field of education, where it has achieved a prominence that many educators find disturbing. Creativity testing owes its existence to World War II, when the air force commissioned J. P. Guilford, a psychologist at the University of Southern California, to study the subject. The air force wanted to select pilots who in an emergency —the unexpected failure of a gear or instrument—would respond with appropriately original behavior, saving themselves and the plane. The usual IQ tests were not The usual IQ tests were not designed to tap originality, and hence Guilford was funded to develop what later became known as the tests for divergent thinking. As mentioned earlier, World War II was especially beneficial for women scientists. Several said that they probably would not have been admitted to graduate school if so many men had not been drafted and the graduate departments had not been looking desperately for qualified students. After graduating, these same women found jobs in government-sponsored research labsinvolvedwiththewareffort labs involved with the war effort, or the later attempts to keep up scientific superiority fueled by the Cold War. Margaret Butler fondly recalls the early postwar years at Argonne, where she became involved with the birth and the infancy of computer science. Those were exciting times, when outside historical events, technological advances, and new scientific discoveries fused into a single stimulus to work hard and tackle important problems. The influence of historical events on the arts is less direct but probablynotlessimportantIt probably not less important. It could be argued, for instance, that the breakaway from classical literary, musical, and artistic styles that is so characteristic of the twentieth century was an indirect reaction to the disillusion people felt at the inability of Western civilization to avoid the bloodshed of World War I. It is no coincidence that Einstein's theory of relativity, Freud's theory of the unconscious, Eliot's free-form poetry, Stravinsky's twelve-tone music, Martha Graham's abstract choreography, Picasso's deformed figures, James Joyce's stream of consciousnessprosewereall consciousness prose were all created—and were accepted by the public—in the same period in which empires collapsed and belief systems rejected old certainties. The Egyptian writer Naguib Mahfouz has spent many decades chronicling imaginatively the forces that are tearing apart the ancient fabric of his culture: colonialism, shifting of values, social mobility that creates new wealth and new poverty, and the changing roles of men and women. His ideas originate: in the process of living. We learn togetonwithlifeevenbeforewe to get on with life even before we think of writing about it. There are particular events that sink deeper into our heart than others. My concerns were always political. Politics attracts me very much. Politics, interpersonal relationships, and love. The oppressed people in society. These were the sort of things that attracted me most. For Nina Gruenenberg, associate editor and editorial columnist for the elite opinion-making weekly Die Zeit, unfolding world events provide a constant stream of problematicissuesHerchallenge problematic issues. Her challenge is to grasp the essential elements of the human conflicts involved, the sociocultural context in which the drama is played out, and then to report concisely her personal impression of the events. In the weeks prior to being interviewed, she had been in Texas covering the World Economic Summit, in London for the NATO summit, and in Russia for a meeting between

German chancellor Helmut Kohl and Russian president Mikhail Gorbachev. You know, I run a weekly newspaperandnormallyIam newspaper, and normally I am very proud Wednesday mornings after the newspaper is out of the machinery, and it's ready and fresh, and I am satisfied with the piece I did. The last time I was very satisfied was after Chancellor Kohl went to the Caucasus and talked with President Gorbachev. This was on Monday, and we returned on Monday evening. I came back here to Hamburg on Tuesday morning, and by that evening the article had to be written. It was the end, it was the event of the week, and so I had to do an articlewhichseemedtomeandto article which seemed to me and to all of my colleagues very important. But I was very tired and exhausted. And so I had really some difficulty in getting it done my way and in concentrating. And after that, the next morning, I was very happy! The creative process starts with a sense that there is a puzzle somewhere, or a task to be accomplished. Perhaps something is not right, somewhere there is a conflict, a tension, a need to be satisfied. The problematic issue can be triggered by a personal experiencebyalackoffitinthe experience, by a lack of fit in the symbolic system, by the stimulation of colleagues, or by public needs. In any case, without such a felt tension that attracts the psychic energy of the person, there is no need for a new response. Therefore, without a stimulus of this sort, the creative process is unlikely to start. PRESENTED AND DISCOVERED PROBLEMS Problems are not all alike in the way they come to a person's attention. Most problems are already formulated; everybody knowswhatistobedoneandonly knows what is to be done and only the solution is missing. The person is expected by employers, patrons, or some other external pressure to apply his or her mind to the solution of a puzzle. These are "presented" problems. But there are also situations in which nobody has asked the question yet, nobody even knows that there is a problem. In this case the creative person identifies both the problem and the solution. Here we have a "discovered" problem. Einstein, among others, believed that the really important breakthroughs in science come as a result of reformulatingoldproblemsor reformulating old problems or discovering new ones, rather than by just solving existing problems. Or as Freeman Dyson said: "It is characteristic of scientific life that it is easy when you have a problem to work on. The hard part is finding your problem." Frank Offner illustrates a presented problem-solving process: When I first was getting into aircraft, I had a best friend who introduced me to Hamilton Standard, who made propellers, now part of United Technology. HesuggestedthatIgoseethem He suggested that I go see them and see if I could help them, and the chief of the vibration group said to me, "Now, Frank, we have had this problem for months, we cannot figure how to get the maximum positive and the maximum negative value of the voltage and take the sum of them and figure out the total stress. We don't know how to choose a resistor. You have to have a capacitor that has to agree with the resistor, because if the resistor is too high it's too sluggish and if it's too low you lose one before you get the other." Well, before he wasfinishedtalkingIknewthe was finished talking I knew the answer. I said, "Don't use a resistor, use a little relay and you short the capacitor..." In contrast, Robert Galvin describes a problem that is discovered. His father had founded Motorola early in the century to make car radios. For several decades the business was a small one-room operation, with perhaps a dozen engineers and no large contracts, so Galvin's father worked very hard to make ends meet. In 1936 he felt that he finally could afford to take a vacation. He tookhiswifeandyoungRobertona took his wife and young Robert on a European tour. As they traveled across Germany, the elder Galvin became convinced that sooner or later Hitler would start a war. Upon his return home, he followed up his hunch by sending Don Mitchell, one of his assistants, to Camp McCoy in Wisconsin to find out how the army passed on information among its various units. Mitchell drove to Wisconsin, rang a bell at the gate of the camp, sat down with the major in charge, and in a short time found out that, as far as communications were concerned, thearmyhadn'tchangedatallsince the army hadn't changed at all since World War I: A phone wire was run from the front line to the back trenches. Upon being told this, Galvin's ears perked up. "Don," he is supposed to have said, "if we can make a radio that fits in a car and receives signals, can't we marry a little transmitter with it, and could we add some kind of power unit and put it into a box so someone could hold it, and he could talk from the front trench to the back trench with radios instead of stringing out the wire?" They figured it was a good idea and went to work. By the time Hitler invaded PolandMotorolawasreadyto Poland, Motorola was ready to produce what became the SCR 536, the walkie-talkie of World War II. Robert Galvin uses this story to illustrate what he means by anticipation and commitment: on the one hand, having the foresight to realize how you could contribute to the future and thereby profit from it, and on the other, to have faith in your intuition and work hard to actualize it. Presented problems usually take a much shorter time to prepare for and to solve than discovered problems. Sometimes the solution appearswiththeimmediacyof appears with the immediacy of Offner's example. Although it may require little time and effort, a novel solution to a presented problem could change the domain in significant ways and therefore be judged creative. Even in the arts, some of the most enduring paintings of the Middle Ages and the Renaissance were ordered by patrons who specified the size of the canvas, how many figures of what kind, the amount of expensive ground lapis lazuli pigment to be used, the weight of gold foil to be used in the frame, down to the smallest detail. Bach turned out a newcantataeveryfewweeksto new cantata every few weeks to satisfy his patron's demands for religious hymns. Such cases show that, when approached with a desire to come up with the best solution, even the most rigidly predefined problems can result in creative outcomes. Nevertheless, discovered problems have a chance to make a larger difference in the way we see the world. An example is Darwin's slow development of the theory of evolution. Darwin was commissioned to travel with the Beagle around the coast of South Americaanddescribethelargely America and describe the largely unrecorded plant and animal life he encountered there. This was not an assignment that required a creative solution, and Darwin did what he was expected to do. But at the same time, he became more and more interested in and then puzzled by subtle differences in otherwise similar species living in what we now would call different ecological niches. He saw the connection between specific physical traits and corresponding environmental opportunities, such as the shape of a bird's beak and the kind of food available. These observations led totheconceptofdifferential to the concept of differential adaptation, which in turn, after many more detailed observations, led to the idea of natural selection and finally to the concept of the evolution of species. The theory of evolution answered a great number of questions, ranging from why do animals look so different from each other to where do men and women come from. But perhaps the most remarkable feature of Darwin's accomplishment was that these questions had not been stated in an answerable form before, and he had to formulate the problemaswellasproposea problem as well as propose a solution to it. Most great changes in a domain share this feature of Darwin's work: They tend to fall toward the discovered rather than the presented end on the continuum of problematic situations. THE MYSTERIOUS TIME After a creative person senses that on the horizon of his or her expertise there is something that does not fit, some problem that might be worth tackling, the process of creativity usually goes underground for a while. The evidenceforincubationcomesfrom evidence for incubation comes from reports of discoveries in which the creator becomes puzzled by an issue and remembers coming to a sudden insight into the nature of a problem, but does not remember any intermediate conscious mental steps. Because of this empty space in between sensing a problem and intuiting its solution, it has been assumed that an indispensable stage of incubation must take place in an interval of the conscious process. Because of its mysterious quality, incubation has often been thought the most creative part of the entire processTheconscioussequences process. The conscious sequences can be analyzed, to a certain extent, by the rules of logic and rationality. But what happens in the "dark" spaces defies ordinary analysis and evokes the original mystery shrouding the work of genius: One feels almost the need to turn to mysticism, to invoke the voice of the Muse as an explanation. Our respondents unanimously agree that it is important to let problems simmer below the threshold of consciousness for a time. One of the most eloquent accounts of the importance of this stagecomesagainfromthe stage comes again from the physicist Freeman Dyson. In describing his current work he has this to say: I am fooling around not doing anything, which probably means that this is a creative period, although of course you don't know until afterward. I think that it is very important to be idle. I mean, they always say that Shakespeare was idle between plays. I am not comparing myself to Shakespeare, but people who keep themselves busy all of the time are generally not creative. SoIamnotashamedofbeing So I am not ashamed of being idle. Frank Offner is equally strong in his belief in the importance of not always thinking about one's problem: I will tell you one thing that I found in both science and technology: If you have a problem, don't sit down and try to solve it. Because I will never solve it if I am just sitting down and thinking about it. It will hit me maybe in the middle of the night, while I am driving my car ortakingashowerorsomething or taking a shower, or something like that. How long a period of incubation is needed varies depending on the nature of the problem. It may range from a few hours to several weeks and even longer. Manfred Eigen says that he goes to sleep every night mulling some unresolved problem in his mind, some experimental procedure that does not work, some laboratory process that is not quite right. Miraculously, when he wakes up in the morning he has the solution clearly in mind. Hazel Henderson jogs or does gardeningwhensherunsdryof gardening when she runs dry of ideas, and when she returns to the computer they usually flow freely again. Elisabeth Noelle-Neumann needs plenty of sleep, otherwise she feels that her thoughts become routine and predictable. Donald Campbell is very clear about the importance of letting ideas make connections with each other without external distractions: One of the values in walking to work is mental meandering. Or if driving, not to have the car radio on. Now I don't think of myself as necessarily especially creative, butthiscreativityhastobea but this creativity has to be a profoundly wasteful process. And that mental meandering, mind wandering and so on, is an essential process. If you are allowing that mentation to be driven by the radio or the television or other people's conversations, you are just cutting down on your exploratory, your intellectual exploratory time. These short periods of incubation, usually having to do with a "presented" problem, tend to result in minuscule, perhaps imperceptible, changes in the domainExamplesofsomewhat domain. Examples of somewhat longer periods of incubation are the few weeks Freeman Dyson spent in California sight-seeing and not thinking consciously at all about how to reconcile Feynman and Schwinger's theories. In general, it seems that the more thorough the revolution brought about by the novelty, the longer it was working its way underground. But this hypothesis is difficult to verify. How long did Einstein's theory of relativity incubate? Or Darwin's theory of evolution? Or Beethoven's ideas for the Fifth Symphony? Because it is impossibletodeterminewith impossible to determine with precision when the first germs of these great works appeared in the minds of their authors, it is also impossible to know how long the process of incubation lasted. The Functions of Idle Time But what happens during this mysterious idle time, when the mind is not consciously preoccupied with the problem? There are several competing explanations of why incubation helps the creative process. Perhaps the best known is an offshoot of psychoanalytic theoryAccordingtoFreudthe theory. According to Freud, the curiosity at the roots of the creative process—especially in the arts—is triggered by a childhood experience of sexual origin, a memory so devastating that it had to be repressed. The creative person is one who succeeds in displacing the quest for the forbidden knowledge into a permissible curiosity. The artist's zeal in trying to find new forms of representation and the scientist's urge to strip away the veils of nature are really disguised attempts to understand the confusing impressions the child felt when witnessing his parents having sex, ortheambivalentlyeroticemotions or the ambivalently erotic emotions toward one of the parents. But if the secondary creative process is to drain effectively the repressed primary interest, it has to dip occasionally below the threshold of consciousness, where it can connect again with its original libidinal source. This is presumably what happens during the period of incubation. The content of the conscious line of thought is taken up by the subconscious, and there, out of reach of the censorship of awareness, the abstract scientific problemhasachancetoreveal problem has a chance to reveal itself for what it is—an attempt to come to terms with a very personal conflict. Refreshed by having been able to commune with its true source, the subconscious thought can then reemerge in consciousness, its disguise back in place, and the scientist can continue his or her research with renewed vigor. Many creative people use a watered-down version of this account to explain their own work and often drop hints as to the probable libidinal origin of their interests. It is difficult to know what tomakeofsuchintelligenceOften to make of such intelligence. Often it turns out that the artists or scientists who are most convinced that in their works they are attempting to resolve a childhood trauma are those who have spent many years in therapy and have been well socialized into Freudian ideology. It could be that analysis helped them uncover the repressed sources of their curiosity. Or it could be that it helped them come up with an interesting explanation for what is mysterious about their experiences—an explanation, however, that may have little basis in reality. In any case, although a psychoanalytic approach might explain some of the motivation for a person to engage in the process of discovery, it provides very little guidance as to why a vacation in California yielded Dyson the key to quantum electrodynamics. The transformation of libido in such a case is so spectacularly implausible as to lack credibility. Cognitive accounts of what happens during incubation assume, like the psychoanalytic ones, that some kind of information processingkeepsgoingoninthe processing keeps going on in the mind even when we are not aware of it, even when we are asleep. The difference is that cognitive theories do not posit any direction to subconscious thought. There is no trauma at the center of the unconscious, seeking resolution through disguised curiosity. Cognitive theorists believe that ideas, when deprived of conscious direction, follow simple laws of association. They combine more or less randomly, although seemingly irrelevant associations between ideas may occur as a result of a prior connection: For example, the GermanchemistAugustKekuléhad German chemist August Kekulé had the insight that the benzene molecule might be shaped like a ring after he fell asleep while watching sparks in the fireplace make circles in the air. If he had stayed awake, Kekulé would have presumably rejected as ridiculous the thought that there might be a connection between the sparks and the shape of the molecule. But in the subconscious, rationality could not censor the connection, and so when he woke up he was no longer able to ignore its possibility. According to this perspective, truly irrelevant connections dissolve and disappear frommemorywhiletheonesthat from memory, while the ones that are robust survive long enough to emerge eventually into consciousness. The distinction between serial and parallel processing of information may also explain what happens during incubation. In a serial system like that of an oldfashioned calculator, a complex numerical problem must be solved in a sequence, one step at a time. In a parallel system such as in advanced computer software, a problem is broken up into its component steps, the partial computationsarecarriedout computations are carried out simultaneously, and then these are reconstituted into a single final solution. Something similar to parallel processing may be taking place when the elements of a problem are said to be incubating. When we think consciously about an issue, our previous *training and the effort to arrive at a solution push our ideas in a linear direction, usually along predictable or familiar lines. But intentionality does not work in the subconscious. Free from rational direction, ideas can combineandpursueeachother combine and pursue each other every which way. Because of this freedom, original connections that would be at first rejected by the rational mind have a chance to become established. The Field, the Domain, and the Unconscious At first sight, incubation seems to occur exclusively within the mind; what's more, within the mind's hidden recesses where consciousness is unable to reach. But after a closer look, we must admit that even in the unconscious thesymbolsystemandthesocial the symbol system and the social environment play important roles. In the first place, it is obvious that incubation cannot work for a person who has not mastered a domain or been involved in a field. A new solution to quantum electrodynamics doesn't occur to a person unfamiliar with this branch of physics, no matter how long he or she sleeps. Even though subconscious thinking may not follow rational lines, it still follows patterns that were established during conscious learning. We internalize the knowledgeofthedomainthe knowledge of the domain, the concerns of the field, and they become part of the way our minds are organized. It is often not necessary to perform an experiment to know that something won't work: Theoretical knowledge can predict the outcome. Similarly, we can predict what our colleagues will say if we express publicly certain ideas. When we sit alone in our study and say that an idea won't work, what we may be saying is that none of the people whose opinions matter will accept it. These internalized criteria of the domain and the field do not disappearwhenthethoughtprocess disappear when the thought process goes underground. They are probably less insistent than when we are aware of what we are doing, but they still shape and control how combinations of ideas are evaluated and selected. But just as one must take the concerns of the discipline seriously, one must also be willing to take a stand against received wisdom, if the conditions warrant it. Otherwise no advance is possible. The allimportant tension between trusting domain knowledge yet being ready to reject it is well illustrated by FrankOffner'sdescriptionofwhat Frank Offner's description of what went on in his mind as he was trying to develop the first electronic controls that eventually made possible the commercial use of jet engines: If you understand science and a question comes up and you want to do something, then you can work out a good solution very easily. If you don't have a good scientific background, you can't. If I had looked at what other people had done before, like in the jet engines, I would have been lost. Everybody attacked it exactlythewrongwayThey exactly the wrong way. They thought the way that I did it was impossible. [Norbert] Weiner, the mathematician—I read his book on cybernetics—that said it was impossible. But I used rate acceleration feedback, and it worked. What Offner points out here is that a creative solution often requires using knowledge from one part of the domain to correct the accepted beliefs of the field—which are based on different conclusions derived from other parts of the same domain. In this case, cybernetictheoryseemedto cybernetic theory seemed to exclude the possibility of controls that would keep the speed of the jet engine exactly constant. But before ever seeing a jet engine, by thinking about what the controls were supposed to accomplish and then going back to basic physics, Offner came up with a design that worked and was implemented. Creative thoughts evolve in this gap filled with tension—holding on to what is known and accepted while tending toward a still illdefined truth that is barely glimpsed on the other side of the chasm. Even whenthoughtsincubatebelowthe when thoughts incubate below the threshold of consciousness, this tension is present. THE"AHA!" EXPERIENCE Most of the people in our sample— but not all—recall with great intensity and precision a particular moment when some major problem crystallized in their minds in such a way that a solution became all but inevitable, requiring only a matter of time and hard work. For presented problems, the insight might even include the particulars of the solution. Here are two examplesfromFrankOffner: examples from Frank Offner: It will hit me maybe in the middle of the night. It turns around somehow inside your brain. I can tell you where I was when I got the answer how to stabilize the jet control with a feedback. I was sitting on a sofa, I guess this was before I was married, at some friend's house and a little bit bored and the answer hit me, "Ah!" and I put in the derivative term. And another one. I was going to do my Ph.D. thesis on nerve excitationTherewereetwosetsof excitation. There were two sets of equations describing nerve excitation. I was going to make some experiments to see which was the right one, one made at the University of Chicago, the other in England, and I was going to see which was the more accurate. And I tried to work out the mathematics to see what kind of experiment would [be decisive]. I remember I was taking a shower when I saw how to solve that problem. I sat down to solve that problem and I found that the equations were just two ways of saying the same thing. So I had to dosomethingelse[forthethesis] do something else [for the thesis]. The insight presumably occurs when a subconscious connection between ideas fits so well that it is forced to pop out into awareness, like a cork held underwater breaking out into the air after it is released. THE 99 PERCENT PERSPIRATION After an insight occurs, one must check it out to see if the connections genuinely make sense. The painter steps back from the canvas to see whetherthecompositionworksthe whether the composition works, the poet rereads the verse with a more critical eye, the scientist sits down to do the calculations or run the experiments. Most lovely insights never go any farther, because under the cold light of reason fatal flaws appear. But if everything checks out, the slow and often routine work of elaboration begins. There are four main conditions that are important during this stage of the process. First of all, the person must pay attention to the developing work, to notice when new ideas, new problems, and new insightsariseoutoftheinteraction insights arise out of the interaction with the medium. Keeping the mind open and flexible is an important aspect of the way creative persons carry on their work. Next, one must pay attention to one's goals and feelings, to know whether the work is indeed proceeding as intended. The third condition is to keep in touch with domain knowledge, to use the most effective techniques, the fullest information, and the best theories as one proceeds. And finally, especially in the later stages of the process, it is important to listen to colleagues in the field. By interacting with others involved withsimilarproblemsitis with similar problems, it is possible to correct a line of solution that is going in the wrong direction, to refine and focus one's ideas, and to find the most convincing mode of presenting them, the one that has the best chance of being accepted. The historian Natalie Davis describes how she feels during the last stage of the creative process, when all that is left is the writing up of the results of her research: If I didn't have affect in a project, if I had lost it or maybe it didn'tlasttoolongitwouldlose didn't last too long, it would lose its spark. I mean, I don't want to do something that I have lost my love for. I think that everybody is perhaps that way, but I am very much that way. It is hard to be creative if you are just doing something doggedly. If I didn't have curiosity, if I felt that my curiosity was limited, then the novelty part of it would be gone. Because it is the curiosity that has often pushed me to think of ways of finding out about something that people thought you could never find out about. Or ways of looking at a subject that have never been lookedatbeforeThat'swhat looked at before. That's what keeps me running back and forth to the library, and just thinking, and thinking, and thinking. Barry Commoner describes the last phases of his work, when he has to write things down, or communicate them to an audience: Some of the work is extremely hard from the point of view of creating a clear statement. For example, in one of my books I wrote a chapter on thermodynamics designed for the lay public. That probably went throughfifteendraftsItwasthe through fifteen drafts. It was the most difficult writing I ever had to do, because it's a very difficult subject to put into ordinary lay terms. And that's one of the things I've done I'm most proud of. I've had engineers tell me that for the first time they had a clear picture of thermodynamics from it. So I enjoy that a great deal. I enjoy communicating. Same with speaking. I do a lot of speaking. And I really enjoy seeing the audience paying attention— listening, understanding it. One thing about creative work is thatit'sneverdoneIndifferent that it's never done. In different words, every person we interviewed said that it was equally true that they had worked every minute of their careers, and that they had never worked a day in all their lives. They experienced even the most focused immersion in extremely difficult tasks as a lark, an exhilarating and playful adventure. It is easy to resent this attitude and see the inner freedom of the creative person as an elite privilege. While the rest of us are struggling at boring jobs, they have theluxuryofdoingwhattheylove the luxury of doing what they love to do, not knowing whether it is work or play. There might be an element of truth in this. But far more important, in my opinion, is the message that the creative person is sending us: You, too, can spend your life doing what you love to do. After all, most of the people we interviewed were not born with a silver spoon in their mouth; many came from humble origins and struggled to create a career that allowed them to keep exploring their interests. Even if we don't have the good fortune to discover a new chemical element or write a greatstorytheloveofthecreative great story, the love of the creative process for its own sake is available to all. It is difficult to imagine a richer life.*

4

Flow of creativity

Creative persons differ from one another in a variety of ways, but in one respect they are unanimous: They all love what they do. It is not the hope of achieving fame or making money that drives them; rather, it is the opportunity to do the work that they enjoy doing. Jacob Rabinow explains: "You invent for thehellofitIdon'tstartwiththe the hell of it. I don't start with the idea, 'What will make money?' This is a rough world; money's important. But if I have to trade between what's fun for me and what's money-making, I'll take what's fun." The novelist Naguib Mahfouz concurs in more genteel tones: "I love my work more than I love what it produces. I am dedicated to the work regardless of its consequences." We found the same sentiments in every single interview. What is extraordinary in this case is that we talked to engineers and chemistswritersandmusicians chemists, writers and musicians, businesspersons and social reformers, historians and architects, sociologists and physicians—and they all agree that they do what they do primarily because it's fun. Yet many others in the same occupations don't enjoy what they do. So we have to assume that it is not what these people do that counts but how they do it. Being an engineer or a carpenter is not in itself enjoyable. But if one does these things a certain way, then they become intrinsically rewarding, worth doing for their own sake. What is the secret of transforming activitiessothattheyarerewarding activities so that they are rewarding in and of themselves? PROGRAMMED FOR CREATIVITY When people are asked to choose from a list the best description of how they feel when doing whatever they enjoy doing most—reading, climbing mountains, playing chess, whatever—the answer most frequently chosen is "designing or discovering something new." At first, it seems strange that dancers, rock climbers, and composers all agree that their most enjoyable experiencesresembleaprocessof experiences resemble a process of discovery. But when we think about it some more, it seems perfectly reasonable that at least some people should enjoy discovering and creating above all else. To see the logic of this, try a simple thought experiment. Suppose that you want to build an organism, an artificial life form, that will have the best chance of surviving in a complex and unpredictable environment, such as that on Earth. You want to build into this organismsome mechanism that will prepare it to confront as many of the sudden dangersandtotakeadvantageofas dangers and to take advantage of as many of the opportunities that arise as possible. How would you go about doing this? Certainly you would want to design an organism that is basically conservative, one that learns the best solutions from the past and keeps repeating them, trying to save energy, to be cautious and go with the tried-and-true patterns of behavior. But the best solution would also include a relay system in a few organisms that would give a positive reinforcement every time they discovered something new or cameupwithanovelideaor came up with a novel idea or behavior, whether or not it was immediately useful. It is especially important to make sure that the organism was not rewarded only for useful discoveries, otherwise it would be severely handicapped in meeting the future. For no earthly builder could anticipate the kind of situations the species of new organisms might encounter tomorrow, next year, or in the next decade. So the best program is one that makes the organism feel good whenever something new is discovered, regardless of its present usefulness. And this is what seemstohavehappenedwithour seems to have happened with our race through evolution. By random mutations, some individuals must have developed a nervous system in which the discovery of novelty stimulates the pleasure centers in the brain. Just as some individuals derive a keener pleasure from sex and others from food, so some must have been born who derived a keener pleasure fromlearning something new. It is possible that children who were more curious ran more risks and so were more likely to die early than their more stolid companions. But it isalsoprobablethatthosehuman is also probable that those human groups that learned to appreciate the curious children among them, and helped to protect and reward them so that they could grow to maturity and have children of their own, were more successful than groups that ignored the potentially creative in their midst. If this is true, we are the descendants of ancestors who recognized the importance of novelty, protected those individuals who enjoyed being creative, and learned from them. Because they had among them individuals who enjoyedexploringandinventing enjoyed exploring and inventing, they were better prepared to face the unpredictable conditions that threatened their survival. So we too share this propensity for enjoying whatever we do, provided we can do it in a new way, provided we can discover or design something new in doing it. This is why creativity, no matter in what domain it takes place, is so enjoyable. This is why Brenda Milner, among many others, said: "I would say that I am impartial about what is important or great, because every new little discovery, even a tiny one, is exciting at the moment of discovery" discovery." But this is only part of the story. Another force motivates us, and it is more primitive and more powerful than the urge to create: the force of entropy. This too is a survival mechanism built into our genes by evolution. It gives us pleasure when we are comfortable, when we relax, when we can get away with feeling good without expending energy. If we didn't have this built-in regulator, we could easily kill ourselves by running ragged and then not having enough reserves of strength, body fat, or nervous energytofacetheunexpected energy to face the unexpected. This is the reason why the urge to relax, to curl up comfortably on the sofa whenever we can get away with it, is so strong. Because this conservative urge is so powerful, for most people "free time" means a chance to wind down, to park the mind in neutral. When there are no external demands, entropy kicks in, and unless we understand what is happening, it takes over our body and our mind. We are generally torn between two opposite sets of instructions programmed into the brain: the least-effort imperative on onesideandtheclaimsof one side, and the claims of creativity on the other. In most individuals entropy seems to be stronger, and they enjoy comfort more than the challenge of discovery. A few, like the ones who tell their stories in this book, are more responsive to the rewards of discovery. But we all respond to both of these rewards; the tendencies toward conserving energy as well as using it constructively are simultaneously part of our inheritance. Which one wins depends not only on our genetic makeup but also presumably onourearlyexperiencesHowever on our early experiences. However, unless enough people are motivated by the enjoyment that comes from confronting challenges, by discovering new ways of being and doing, there is no evolution of culture, no progress in thought or feeling. It is important, therefore, to understand better what enjoyment consists of and how creativity can produce it. WHAT IS ENJOYMENT? In order to answer that question, many years ago I started to study people who seemed to be doing thingsthattheyenjoyedbutwere things that they enjoyed but were not rewarded for with money or fame. Chess players, rock climbers, dancers, and composers devoted many hours a week to their avocations. Why were they doing it? It was clear from talking to them that what kept them motivated was the quality of experince they felt when they were involved with the activity. This feeling didn't come when they were relaxing, when they were taking drugs or alcohol, or when they were consuming the expensive privileges of wealth. Rather, it often involved painful, risky, difficult activities that stretchedtheperson'scapacityand stretched the person's capacity and involved an element of novelty and discovery. This optimal experience is what I have called flow, because many of the respondents described the feeling when things were going well as an almost automatic, effortless, yet highly focused state of consciousness. The flow experience was described in almost identical terms regardless of the activity that produced it. Athletes, artists, religious mystics, scientists, and ordinary working people described their most rewarding experiences withverysimilarwordsAndthe with very similar words. And the description did not vary much by culture, gender, or age; old and young, rich and poor, men and women, Americans and Japanese seem to experience enjoyment in the same way, even though they may be doing very different things to attain it. Nine main elements were mentioned over and over again to describe how it feels when an experience is enjoyable. 1. There are clear goals every step of the way. In contrast to what happens in everyday life, on the job or at home, where often therearecontradictorydemands there are contradictory demands and our purpose is unsure, in flow we always know what needs to be done. The musician knows what notes to play next, the rock climber knows the next moves to make. When a job is enjoyable, it also has clear goals: The surgeon is aware how the incision should proceed moment by moment; the farmer has a plan for how to carry out the planting. 2. There is immediate feedback to one's actions. Again, in contrast to the usual state of affairs, in a flow experience we knowhowwellwearedoing know how well we are doing. The musician hears right away whether the note played is the one. The rock climber finds out immediately whether the move was correct because he or she is still hanging in there and hasn't fallen to the bottom of the valley. The surgeon sees there is no blood in the cavity, and the farmer sees the furrows lining up neatly in the field. 3. There is a balance between challenges and skills. In flow, we feel that our abilities are well matched to the opportunities for actionIneverydaylifewe action. In everyday life we sometimes feel that the challenges are too high in relation to our skills, and then we feel frustrated and anxious. Or we feel that our potential is greater than the opportunities to express it, and then we feel bored. Playing tennis or chess against a much better opponent leads to frustration; against a much weaker opponent, to boredom. In a really enjoyable game, the players are balanced on the fine line between boredom and anxiety. The same is true when work, or a conversation, or a relationship is going well. 4. Action and awareness are merged. It is typical of everyday experience that our minds are disjointed from what we do. Sitting in class, students may appear to be paying attention to the teacher, but they are actually thinking about lunch, or last night's date. The worker thinks about the weekend; the mother cleaning house is worried about her child; the golfer's mind is preoccupied with how his swing looks to his friends. In flow, however, our concentration is focused on what we do. Onepointednessofmindisrequired pointedness of mind is required by the close match between challenges and skills, and it is made possible by the clarity of goals and the constant availability of feedback. 5. Distractions are excluded from consciousness. Another typical element of flow is that we are aware only of what is relevant here and now. If the musician thinks of his health or tax problems when playing, he is likely to hit a wrong note. If the surgeon's mind wanders during an operation, the patient's life is in dangerFlowistheresultof danger. Flow is the result of intense concentration on the present, which relieves us of the usual fears that cause depression and anxiety in everyday life. 6. There is no worry of failure. While in flow, we are too involved to be concerned with failure. Some people describe it as a feeling of total control; but actually we are not in control, it's just that the issue does not even come up. If it did, we would not be concentrating totally, because our attention would be split between what we did and the feelingofcontrolThereasonthat feeling of control. The reason that failure is not an issue is that in flow it is clear what has to be done, and our skills are potentially adequate to the challenges. 7. Self-consciousness disappears. In everyday life, we are always monitoring how we appear to other people; we are on the alert to defend ourselves from potential slights and anxious to make a favorable impression. Typically this awareness of self is a burden. In flow we are too involved in what we are doing to careaboutprotectingtheegoYet care about protecting the ego. Yet after an episode of flow is over, we generally emerge from it with a stronger self-concept; we know that we have succeeded in meeting a difficult challenge. We might even feel that we have stepped out of the boundaries of the ego and have become part, at least temporarily, of a larger entity. The musician feels at one with the harmony of the cosmos, the athlete moves at one with the team, the reader of a novel lives for a few hours in a different reality. Paradoxically, the self expands through acts of selfforgetfulness forgetfulness. 8. The sense of time becomes distorted. Generally in flow we forget time, and hours may pass by in what seem like a few minutes. Or the opposite happens: A figure skater may report that a quick turn that in real time takes only a second seems to stretch out for ten times as long. In other words, clock time no longer marks equal lengths of experienced time; our sense of how much time passes depends on what we are doing. 9. The activity becomes autotelicWhenevermostofthese autotelic. Whenever most of these conditions are present, we begin to enjoy whatever it is that produces such an experience. I may be scared of using a computer and learn to do it only because my job depends on it. But as my skills increase, and I recognize what the computer allows me to do, I may begin to enjoy using the computer for its own sake as well. At this point the activity becomes autotelic, which is Greek for something that is an end in itself. Some activities such as art, music, and sports are usually autotelic: There is no reasonfordoingthemexceptto reason for doing them except to feel the experience they provide. Most things in life are exotelic. We do them not because we enjoy them but in order to get at some later goal. And some activities are both: The violinist gets paid for playing, and the surgeon gets status and good money for operating, as well as getting enjoyment from doing what they do. In many ways, the secret to a happy life is to learn to get flow from as many of the things we have to do as possible. If work and family life become autotelic, then there is nothing wasted in lifeandeverythingwedois life, and everything we do is worth doing for its own sake. THE CONDITIONS FOR FLOW IN CREATIVITY Creativity involves the production of novelty. The process of discovery involved in creating something new appears to be one of the most enjoyable activities any human can be involved in. In fact, it is easy to recognize the conditions of flow in the accounts of our respondents, as they describe how it feels to do the sort of things they do. The Clarity of Goals In certain conditions, the creative process begins with the goal of solving a problem that is given to the person by someone else or is suggested by the state of the art in the domain. Moreover, anything that does not work as well as it could can provide a clear goal to the inventor. This is what Frank Offner describes: Oh, I love to solve problems. If it is why our dishwasher does not work, or why the automobile does notworkorhowthenerve not work, or how the nerve works, or anything. Now I am working on how the hair cells work, and ah…it is so very interesting. I don't care what kind of problem it is. If I can solve it, it is fun. It is really a lot of fun to solve problems, isn't it? Isn't that what is interesting in life? Especially if people say one thing and you show that they have been wrong for twenty years and you can solve it in five minutes. Or the goal may emerge as a problem in the domain—a gap in the network of knowledge, a contradictionamongthefindingsa contradiction among the findings, a puzzling result. Here the goal is to restore harmony in the system by reconciling the apparent disparities. The physicist Viktor Weisskopf describes the enjoyment involved in this process: Well, in science, obviously, if I understand something, you know, a new discovery, it need not be my own, a discovery of somebody else, where I say, "Aha, now I understand natural processes that I did not understand before," that is the joy of insight. In music it is the insight into whatthepiecemeansWhatit what the piece means. What it tells you, what the composer wanted to tell you, the beauty or expression or religious feelings, things like that. For artists the goal of the activity is not so easily found. In fact, the more creative the problem, the less clear it is what needs to be done. Discovered problems, the ones that generate the greatest changes in the domain, are also the most difficult to enjoy working on because of their elusiveness. In such cases, the creative person somehow must develop an unconscious mechanism thattellshimorherwhattodoThe that tells him or her what to do. The poet György Faludy usually does not start writing until a "voice" tells him, often in the middle of the night, "György, it's time to start writing." He adds ruefully: "That voice has my number, but I don't have his." The ancients called that voice the Muse. Or it can be a vision, as it is for Robertson Davies: You are always writing, and you're always fantasizing. What I find very much in my own work, though I don't know if it applies to the work of other people, is that an idea for a novel seizes me andwillnotletmegountilIhave and will not let me go until I have given it careful consideration. And that is not to say that a complete story appears in my head, but very often what appears is a picture which seems somehow significant and which must be considered. Now, a great many years ago, I found that whenever I stopped thinking about something in particular, a picture kept coming up in my head. It was a picture of a street, and I knew what street it was; it was the street on which I was born in a small Ontario village. And there were two boys playing in the snowandonethrewasnowball snow, and one threw a snowball at the other. Readers of Davies's oeuvre will recognize in this picture the opening scene of Fifth Business, the first volume of his famous Deptford trilogy. In many ways, the writing of the book consisted in finding out what that image, charged with emotion and nostalgia, portended. The goal was to find out what were the consequences of throwing that snowball. Probably if Davies had told himself rationally that this is what the book would be about he would have thought it a trivial goal, notworthallthetimeandeffort not worth all the time and effort. But fortunately the goal presented itself as a vision, a mysterious call that he felt impelled to follow. Very often this is how the Muse communicates—through a glass darkly, as it were. It is a splendid arrangement, for if the artist were not tricked by the mystery, he or she might never venture into the unexplored territory. Knowing How Well One Is Doing Games are designed so that we can keep score and know how well we are doing. Most jobs give some sort ofinformationaboutperformance: of information about performance: The salesman can add up daily sales, the assembly worker can count pieces produced. If all else fails, the boss may tell you how well you are doing. But the artist, the scientist, and the inventor are moving on very different timelines. How do they know, day in and day out, whether they are wasting their time or actually accomplishing something? This is indeed a difficult problem. Many artists give up because it is just too excruciating to wait until critics or galleries take notice and passjudgmentontheircanvases pass judgment on their canvases. Research scientists drift away from pure science because they cannot tolerate the long cycles of insecurity before reviewers and editors evaluate their results. So how can they experience flow without external information about their performance? The solution seems to be that those individuals who keep doing creative work are those who succeed in internalizing the field's criteria of judgment to the extent that they can give feedback to themselves, without having to wait tohearfromexpertsThepoetwho to hear from experts. The poet who keeps enjoying writing verse is the one who knows how good each line is, how appropriate is each word chosen. The scientist who enjoys her work is the one who has a sense of what a good experiment is like and who appreciates it when a test is well run or when a report is clearly written. Then she need not wait until October to see if her name is on the Nobel Prize list. Many creative scientists say that the difference between them and their less creative peers is the ability to separate bad ideas from goodonessothattheydon'twaste good ones, so that they don't waste much time exploring blind alleys. Everyone has both bad and good ideas all the time, they say. But some people can't tell them apart until it's too late, until they have already invested a great deal of time in the unprofitable hunches. This is another form of the ability to give oneself feedback: to know in advance what is feasible and what will work, without having to suffer the consequences of bad judgment. At Linus Pauling's sixtieth birthday celebration, a student asked him, "Dr. Pauling, how does one go about having good ideas?" He replied"Youhavealotofideas replied, "You have a lot of ideas and throw away the bad ones." To do that, of course, one has to have a very well internalized picture of what the domain is like and what constitutes "good" and "bad" ideas according to the field. Balancing Challenges and Skills The pursuit of a creative problem is rarely easy. In fact, in order to be enjoyable it should be hard, and of course so it is, almost by definition. It is never easy to break new ground, to venture into the unknown. When one starts out, the difficulties mayseemalmostoverwhelming may seem almost overwhelming. Here is how Freeman Dyson describes this aspect of the process: Well, I think that you have to describe it as sort of a struggle. I have to always force myself to write, and also to work harder at a science problem. You have to put blood, sweat, and tears into it first. And it is awfully hard to get started. I think most writers have this problem. I mean, it's part of the business. You may work very hard for a week producing the first page. That's really blood, tears, and sweat, and there is nothingelsetodescribeitYou nothing else to describe it. You have to force yourself to push and push and push with the hope that something good will come out. And you have to go through that process before it really starts to flow easily, and without that preliminary forcing and pushing probably nothing would ever happen. So, I think that is what distinguishes it from just having a good time—you have a good time once you are really in the flowing phase, but you have to overcome some sort of barrier to get there. That is why I say it is unconscious, because you don't knowactuallywhetheryouare know actually whether you are really getting anywhere or not. In that phase it just seems to be unadulterated torture. The creative person is not immune to the conflict between the two programs we all carry in our genetic inheritance. As Dyson knows, even the most creative persons must overcome the barrier of entropy. It is impossible to accomplish something that is truly new and worthwhile without struggling with it. It isn't just in competitive sports that the saying "no pain, no gain" applies.

The less welldefinedtheproblemthemore well defined the problem, the more ambitious it is, and the harder it is for the creative person to get a handle on it. Barry Commoner points out: I enjoy doing things that other people won't do. Because what are they? They're usually things that are difficult and important— and that people shy away from. I have a general approach to thinking of the way in which issues develop. I'm interested in the origins of problems. And so I have a pretty good idea of where things are going, and what's importantandwhatisn't important and what isn't important. And I try very hard to be at the cutting edge of problems. Very often that puts me so far out in front that people are upset about it, but that's OK. To be able to cope with such problems, the creative person has to have a great many personality traits that are conducive to discovery and hard work, including the ability to internalize the rules of the domain and the judgments of the field. Commoner also gives a hint of another skill that creative individuals develop: a personal approachaninternalmodelthat approach, an internal model that allows them to put the problem into a manageable context. The same idea is expressed by Linus Pauling: I think one thing that I do is to bring ideas from one field of knowledge into another field of knowledge. And, I've often said I don't think that I'm smarter than a lot of other scientists, but perhaps I think more about the problems. I have a picture, a sort of general theory of the universe in my mind that I've built up over the decades. If I read an article, or hear someone give a seminar talk, orinsomeotherwaygetsome or in some other way get some piece of information about science that I hadn't had before, I ask myself, "How does that fit into my picture of the universe?" and if it doesn't fit, I ask, "Why doesn't it fit in?" The strategies creative individuals develop are not always successful. They take risks, and what is risk without an occasional failure? When the challenges become too great for the person to cope with, a sense of frustration rather than joy creeps in—at least for a while. Our interview with JohnReedtookplaceafewyears John Reed took place a few years after Citicorp was bloodied in the market; its shares lost a great deal of their value almost overnight. Reed blamed himself for not foreseeing the contingency that caused the loss. As a result, at the time he felt that some of the fun had gone out of his job. What used to be spontaneous turned into hard work; he had to force himself to be more of an accountant than a builder and leader; and the new skill he had to acquire required unfamiliar discipline. The Merging of Action and Awareness Awareness But when the challenges are just right, the creative process begins to hum, and all other concerns are temporarily shelved in the deep involvement with the activity. Here is Dyson again, describing how it feels after the initial struggle is over: I always find that when I am writing, it is really the fingers that are doing it and not the brain. Somehow the writing takes charge. And the same thing happens of course with equations. Youdon'treallythinkofwhatyou You don't really think of what you are going to write. You just scribble, the equations lead the way, and what you are doing is sort of architectural. You have to have a design in view, in which you design a chapter, or a proof of a theorem, as the case may be. Then you have to put it together out of words or out of symbols as the case may be, but if you don't have a clear architecture in mind then the thing won't end up being any good. The trick is to start from both ends and to meet in the middle, which is essentially like building a bridge. That seems to methewaythatIthinkanyhow me the way that I think, anyhow. So the original design is somehow accidental and you don't know how it comes into your head. It just sort of happens, maybe when you are shaving or taking a walk, then you sit down and actually work through and that is when the hard work is done. And that is very largely a matter of putting pieces together, finding out what works and what doesn't. Barry Commoner uses similar terms to describe the almost automatic quality of the flow experience when writing, expressingthefeelingofmerging expressing the feeling of merging action and awareness through the image of the flowing ink and the flowing of ideas: I write with this pen [he removes a fountain pen from his breast pocket and holds it up]. And it's very clear to me that my ability to think and write at the same time depends on the flow of ink. The thing I enjoy most is the flow of my own ideas and getting them down on paper. I will not write with a ballpoint pen, because it doesn't really flow. That's why I use a fountain pen. Andonlyafountainpenthat And only a fountain pen that really works very well. The novelist Richard Stern gives a classic description of how it feels to become lost in the process of writing and to feel the rightness of one's actions in terms of what is happening in that special world of one's own creation: At your best you're not thinking, How am I making my way ahead in the world by doing this? No. You're concentrated on your characters, on the situation, on the form of the book, on the words whicharecomingoutAndtheir which are coming out. And their shape. You've lost...you're not an ego at that point. It's not competitive. It's...I would use the word pure. You know that this is right. I don't mean that it works in the world, or that it adds up, but that it's right in this place. In this story. It belongs to it. It's right for that person, that character. Avoiding

Distractions Many of the peculiarities attributed to creative persons are really just ways to protect the focus of concentration so that they may lose themselvesinthecreativeprocess themselves in the creative process. Distractions interrupt flow, and it may take hours to recover the peace of mind one needs to get on with the work. The more ambitious the task, the longer it takes to lose oneself in it, and the easier it is to get distracted. A scientist working on an arcane problem must detach himself from the "normal" world and roam with his mind in a world of disembodied symbols that now you see, now you don't. Any intrusion from the solid world of everyday reality can make that world disappear in an instant. It is for this reason that Freeman Dyson "hides"inthelibrarywhenhe's "hides" in the library when he's writing and why Marcel Proust used to seclude himself in a windowless room lined with cork when he sat down to write À la recherche du temps perdu. Even the slightest noise could break the thread of his teetering imagination. More serious health, family, or financial problems could occupy the mind of a person so insistently that he or she is no longer able to devote enough attention to work. Then a long period of drought may follow, a writer's block, a burnout, which may even end a creative careerItisthiskindofdistraction career. It is this kind of distraction that Jacob Rabinow talks about: Freedom from worry is one thing—that you don't have any problem of health or sickness in the family or something that occupies your mind. Or financial worries, that you're going crazy about how you're going to pay the next bill. Or children's worries, or drugs or something. No, it's nice to be free of responsibility. That doesn't mean you have no responsibility to the project, but to be free of other things. And you're not likely to be an inventor ifyou'reverysickYou'retoo if you're very sick. You're too busy with your problems, too many pains. Many of our respondents were thankful to their spouses for providing a buffer from exactly these kinds of distractions. This was especially true of the men; the women sometimes mentioned pointedly that they also would have liked to have had a wife to spare them from worries that interfered with their concentration on work. Forgetting Self, Time, and Surroundings When distractions are out of the way and the other conditions for flow are in place, the creative process acquires all the dimensions of flow. Here it is described by the poet Mark Strand: Well, you're right in the work, you lose your sense of time, you're completely enraptured, you're completely caught up in what you're doing, and you're sort of swayed by the possibilities you see in this work. If that becomes too powerful, then you get up, because the excitement istoogreatYoucan'tcontinueto is too great. You can't continue to work or continue to see the end of the work because you're jumping ahead of yourself all the time. The idea is to be so...so saturated with it that there's no future or past, it's just an extended present in which you're, uh, making meaning. And dismantling meaning, and remaking it. Without undue regard for the words you're using. It's meaning carried to a high order. It's not just essential communication, daily communication; it's a total communication. When you're working on something and you're workingwellyouhavethe working well, you have the feeling that there's no other way of saying what you're saying. He captures precisely the sense of flowing along this extended present and the powerful sense of doing exactly the right thing the only way it could be done. It may not happen often, but when it does the beauty of it justifies all the hard work. Creativity as Autotelic Experience This then brings us back to where we started this chapter and the observationthatallofthe observation that all of the respondents placed the joy of working ahead of any extrinsic rewards they may receive from it. Like most of the others, the psychologist Donald Campbell gives unambiguous advice to young people entering the field: I would say: "Don't go into science if you are interested in money. Don't go into science if you will not enjoy it even if you do not become famous. Let fame be something that you accept graciously if you get it, but make sure that it is a career that you can enjoyThatrequiresintrinsic enjoy. That requires intrinsic motivation. And try to pick a setting in which you can work on the problems that intrinsically motivate you even if they are not exciting to others. Try to have the situational setting so that you can enjoy that work intrinsically, even if you are out of step with the time." Scientists often describe the autotelic aspects of their work as the exhilaration that comes from the pursuit of truth and of beauty. What they seem to describe, however, is the joy of discovery, of solving a problemofbeingabletoexpress problem, of being able to express an observed relationship in a simple and elegant form. So what is rewarding is not a mysterious and ineffable external goal but the activity of science itself. It is the pursuit that counts, not the attainment. Of course this distinction is to a certain extent misleading, because without occasional successes the scientist might become discouraged. But what makes science intrinsically rewarding is the everyday practice, not the rare success. This is how Subrahmanyan Chandrasekhar, the Nobel laureate physicist, describes hisownmotivation: his own motivation: There are two things about me which people generally don't know. I've never worked in anything which is glamorous in any sense. That's point number one. Point number two: I have always worked in areas which, during the time I have worked on them, did not attract attention. The word success is an ambiguous word. Success with respect to the outside? Or success with respect to oneself? And if it is a success with respect to the outsidethenhowdoyouevaluate outside, then how do you evaluate it? Very often outside success is irrelevant, wrong, and misplaced. So how can one talk about it? Externally, you may think I am successful because people write about some aspects of my work. But that is an external judgment. And I have no idea as to how to value that judgment. Success is not one of my motives. Because success stands in contrast to failure. But no worthwhile effort in one's life is either a success or a failure. What do you mean by success? You take aproblemandyouwanttosolve a problem and you want to solve it. Well, if you solve it, in a limited sense it is a success. But it may be a trivial problem. So a judgment about success is not something about which I've ever been serious about in any sense whatever. Certainly all of these people seem to have heeded their own advice. None pursued money and fame. Some became comfortably wealthy from their inventions or their books, but none of them felt fortunate because of it. What they felt fortunate about was that they could getpaidforsomethingtheyhadsuch get paid for something they had such fun doing and that in the bargain they could feel that what they did might help the human condition along. It is indeed lucky to be able to justify one's life activity with words such as those of C. Vann Woodward, who explains why he writes history: It interests me. It is a source of satisfaction. Achieving something that one thinks is important. Without such a consciousness or motivation it seems to me that life could be rather dull and purposeless, and I wouldn't want toattemptthatkindoflifeOf to attempt that kind of life. Of complete leisure, say, of having absolutely nothing to do that one felt was worth doing—that strikes me as a rather desperate situation to be in. FLOW AND HAPPINESS What is the relation between flow and happiness? This is a very interesting and delicate question. At first, it is easy to conclude that the two must be the same thing. But actually the connection is a bit more complex. First of all, when we are in flow, we do not usually feel happyforthesimplereasonthat happy—for the simple reason that in flow we feel only what is relevant to the activity. Happiness is a distraction. The poet in the middle of writing or the scientist working out equations does not feel happy, at least not without losing the thread of his or her thought. It is only after we get out of flow, at the end of a session or in moments of distraction within it, that we might indulge in feeling happy. And then there is the rush of well-being, of satisfaction that comes when the poem is completed or the theorem is proved. In the long runthemoreflowweexperiencein run, the more flow we experience in daily life, the more likely we are to feel happy overall. But this also depends on what activity provides flow. Unfortunately, many people find the only challenges they can respond to are violence, gambling, random sex, or drugs. Some of these experiences can be enjoyable, but these episodes of flow do not add up to a sense of satisfaction and happiness over time. Pleasure does not lead to creativity, but soon turns into addiction—the thrall of entropy. So the link between flow and happinessdependsonwhetherthe happiness depends on whether the flow-producing activity is complex, whether it leads to new challenges and hence to personal as well as cultural growth. Thus we might conclude that all our respondents must be happy, because they do enjoy their work, and their work is certainly complex. But there are further complications to consider. For instance, what if a person enjoyed being a physicist for thirty years, and then found out that his work resulted in a nuclear device that killed millions of people? How would Jonas Salk have felt if his vaccine, instead of saving lives, hadbeenusedbyothersfor had been used by others for biological warfare? Certainly these are not idle questions in today's world, and they suggest that it is possible for complex activities that produce flow to cause long-range unhappiness. Yet when all is said and done, it is much easier to be happy when one's life has been enjoyable. FLOW AND THE EVOLUTION OF CONSCIOUSNESS There are many things that people enjoy: the pleasures of the body, power and fame, material possessionsSomeenjoycollecting possessions. Some enjoy collecting different beer bottles, and a few even enjoy causing pain to themselves or to others. Strangely enough, even though the means to obtain it are widely different, the resulting feeling of well-being is very much the same. Does that mean that all forms of enjoyment are equally worth pursuing? Twenty-five centuries ago, Plato wrote that the most important task for a society was to teach the young to find pleasure in the right objects. Now Plato was conservative even for his times, so he had rather definiteideasaboutwhatthose definite ideas about what those "right things" were that young people should learn to enjoy. We are much too sophisticated in this day and age to have strong feelings in the matter. Yet we probably agree that we would feel better if our children learned to enjoy cooperation rather than violence; reading rather than stealing; chess rather than dice; hiking rather than watching television. In other words, no matter how relativistic and tolerant we have become, we still have priorities. And we do want the next generation to share those priorities. Finally, many of us suspectthatthenextgenerationwill suspect that the next generation will not preserve what we value unless they now enjoy it to some extent. The problem is that it is easier to find pleasure in things that are easier, in activities like sex and violence that are already programmed into our genes. Hunting, fishing, eating, and mating have privileged places in our nervous system. It is also easy to enjoy making money, or discovering new lands, or conquering new territories, or building elaborate palaces, temples, or tombs because these projects are in synchrony with survivalstrategiesestablishedlong survival strategies established long ago in our physiological makeup. It is much more difficult to learn to enjoy doing things that were discovered recently in our evolution, like manipulating symbolic systems by doing math or science or writing poetry or music, and learning from doing these things about the world and about ourselves. Children grow up believing that football players and rock singers must be happy and envy the stars of the entertainment world for what they think must be fabulous, fulfillinglivesAskedwhatthey fulfilling lives. Asked what they would like to do when they grow up, most of them would choose to be athletes and entertainers. They don't realize until much later, if at all, that the glamour of those lives is vulgar tinsel, that to be like them leads anywhere but to happiness. Neither parents nor schools are very effective at teaching the young to find pleasure in the right things. Adults, themselves often deluded by infatuation with fatuous models, conspire in the deception. They make serious tasks seem dull and hard, and frivolous ones exciting andeasySchoolsgenerallyfailto and easy. Schools generally fail to teach how exciting, how mesmerizingly beautiful science or mathematics can be; they teach the routine of literature or history rather than the adventure. It is in this sense that creative individuals live exemplary lives. They show how joyful and interesting complex symbolic activity is. They have struggled through marshes of ignorance, deserts of disinterest, and with the help of parents and a few visionary teachers they have found themselves on the other side of the known. They havebecomepioneersofculture have become pioneers of culture, models for what men and women of the future will be—if there is to be a future at all. It is by following their example that human consciousness will grow beyond the limitations of the past, the programs that genes and cultures have wired into our brains. Perhaps our children, or their children, will feel more joy in writing poetry and solving theorems than in being passively entertained. The lives of these creative individuals reassure us that it is not impossible.

87

5
Make Creative Surroundings

———❦———

Even the most abstract mind is affected by the surroundings of the body. No one is immune to the impressions that impinge on the senses from the outside. Creative individuals may seem to disregard their environment and work happily in even the most dismal surroundings: Michelangelo contortedonhisscaffoldbelowthe contorted on his scaffold below the Sistine ceiling, the Curies freezing in their shabby Parisian lab, and an infinitude of poets scribbling away in dingy rented rooms. But in reality, the spatiotemporal context in which creative persons live has consequences that often go unnoticed. The right milieu is important in more ways than one. It can affect the production of novelty as well as its acceptance; therefore, it is not surprising that creative individuals tend to gravitate toward centers of vital activity, where their work has the chance of succeeding. From time immemorial artists, poetsscholarsandscientistshave poets, scholars, and scientists have sought out places of natural beauty expecting to be inspired by the majestic peaks or the thundering sea. But in the last analysis, what sets creative individuals apart is that regardless of whether the conditions in which they find themselves are luxurious or miserable, they manage to give their surroundings a personal pattern that echoes the rhythm of their thoughts and habits of action. Within this environment of their own making, they can forget the rest of the world and concentrate on pursuing the Muse. BEING IN THE RIGHT PLACE The great centers of learning and commerce have always acted as magnets for ambitious individuals who wanted to leave their mark on the culture. From the Middle Ages onward, master craftsmen traveled all over Europe to build cathedrals and palaces, attracted now by the wealth of one city, then by that of another. Milanese stonemasons built fortresses for Teutonic knights in Poland; Venetian architects and painters went to decorate the courts of the tsars of Russia. Even Leonardothatparagonof Leonardo, that paragon of creativity, kept serving one master after another depending on whether duke, pope, or king could best finance his dreams. The place where one lives is important for three main reasons. The first is that one must be in a position to access the domain in which one plans to work. Information is not distributed evenly in space but is clumped in different geographical nodes. In the past, when the diffusion of information was slower, one went to Göttingen to study some branches ofphysicstoCambridgeor of physics, to Cambridge or Heidelberg for others. Even with our dazzling electronic means for exchanging information, New York is still the best place for an aspiring artist to find out firsthand what's happening in the art world, what future trends other artists are talking about now. But New York is not the best place to learn oceanography, or economics, or astronomy. Iowa might be the place to learn creative writing or etching, and one can learn things about neural networks in Pittsburgh that one cannot learn anywhere else. People in our sample often moved toplaceswhereinformationof to places where information of interest was stored: Subrahmanyan Chandrasekhar took a boat from India to study physics at Cambridge; Freeman Dyson joined Richard Feynman at Cornell; Nina Holton went to Rome to learn bronze casting techniques. Sometimes it is not the person who chooses the place to further his or her knowledge: The opportunities for learning that a place offers capture the person's interest, and involvement with the domain follows. Brenda Milner happened to be in Montreal when the neurophysiologist D. O. Hebb startedtoteachatMcGill started to teach at McGill University. She was so impressed by his seminars that both she and her husband changed the direction of their research, and she became one of the pioneers of the field. Margaret Butler found herself at the Argonne National Laboratories when computers were first put to use in biochemical research, and her lifelong interest in this domain was started by the opportunity to be a pioneer in this area. Rosalyn Yalow became interested in nuclear medicine because she happened to be where the instruments that made such studies possible were availableOfcourseitisnotthat available. Of course, it is not that knowledge is stored in the place; rather it resides in an institution, a local tradition, or a particular person who happens to live in that place. To learn to cast bronze it helps to see how the old Italian craftsmen do it, and if one wanted to learn psychology from Hebb, one just had to go to Montreal. The second reason why a place may help creativity is that novel stimulation is not evenly distributed. Certain environments have a greater density of interaction and provide more excitement and a greatereffervescenceofideas; greater effervescence of ideas; therefore, they prompt the person who is already inclined to break away from conventions to experiment with novelty more readily than if he or she had stayed in a more conservative, more repressive setting. The young artists who were drawn to Paris from all over the world at the end of the last century lived in a heady atmosphere where new ideas, new expressions, and new ways of living constantly jostled one another and called forth further novelty. The novelist Richard Stern describes how an artist may depend on such variety forhisinspiration: for his inspiration: I yearned to go abroad when I was young, reading Hemingway, Fitzgerald, and so on. And once I went there it was extremely exciting for me to become a new personality, to be detached from everything that bound me, noticing everything that was different. That noticing of difference was very important. The languages, even though I was no good at them, were very important. How things were said that were different, the different formulas. Extremely exciting to me. The first time I wentabroadIwastwentyoneI went abroad, I was twenty-one, I began to keep the journal which I've still kept. I would keep it mostly not to go a little nuts— because there's so much that comes in. If I can get it down, then I don't have to worry about it. So being abroad has been very important in that way too. For a theoretical physicist like Freeman Dyson, the stimulation of colleagues in neighboring offices is indispensable. Science, even more than art, is a collective enterprise where information grows much faster in "hot spots" where the thoughtofonepersonbuildsonthat thought of one person builds on that of many others. And then there are places that inhibit the generation of novelty. According to some, universities are too committed to their primary function, which is the preservation of knowledge, to be very good at stimulating creativity. Here Anthony Hecht comments on the pros and cons of this position from a poet's perspective, but his argument applies to other domains as well: There have been a number of poets in modern times who've said poets who teach in the academiesendupbeingdryas academies end up being dry as dust, unimaginative and without daring and all that sort of stuff. I don't think that's true. The academy is neutral; it can, if you want to let it, curtail your imagination, but it doesn't have to. It's a place where you do a certain kind of work and live with certain kinds of people. The kind of people that you live with are pretty good on the whole. They're interesting, quirky, imaginative, idiosyncratic, lively, controversial. And I find that pleasant. I know this would not be the case if I were in a business organizationwhereeverybody's organization where everybody's trying much more eagerly to conform. Finally, access to the field is not evenly distributed in space. The centers that facilitate the realization of novel ideas are not necessarily the ones where the information is stored or where the stimulation is greatest. Often sudden availability of money at a certain place attracts artists or scientists to an otherwise barren environment, and that place *becomes, at least for a while, one of the centers of the field. When in the 1890s William R. Harper was able to convince John D. Rockefeller, flush with dollars made in the oil fields, to part with a few million to start a university in the cornfields south of Chicago, he almost immediately attracted a number of leading scholars from the Northeast who flocked to the wilderness and established a great center of research and scholarship. Eighty years later the same phenomenon repeated itself farther west, when oil money made it possible for the University of Texas to attract a new generation of intellectual leaders to Austin. Oil is just one source of financial lure that greases the movement of academic fields from one place to another. After luminaries settle down in a particular place, it becomes difficult for young people with similar interests to resist their attraction. George Stigler, member of a department that has collected more Nobel Prizes in economics than any other in the world, explains some of the reasons why this is so: The intellectual atmosphere in which you are determines a lot how you work. And Chicago in economics has been a virile, challenging, aggressive, and political environment. You're surrounded by able colleagues who are quite willing to embarrass you a little if you're doing something that's foolish or wrong but are quite willing to help you, too, on things that have promise, so that it's an extremely helpful environment. The career of John Bardeen is typical. He went to graduate school at Princeton, where he became the second doctoral student of Eugene Wigner, a distinguished theoretical physicist who was awarded the Nobel Prize in 1963. Not surprisingly, many of Wigner's students also became leaders in the field. Bardeen then went to work at the Bell Research Laboratories, where many of the bright young physicists were being hired. This is how he describes the atmosphere there: Bell Labs had a really outstanding group in solid-state theory. The way the organization was designed, they didn't have a theoretical group as such, but the theorists had their offices in close proximity so that they could talk readily with one another but they'd report to different experimental groups. So there was very close interaction between theory and experiment, and most papers were coauthored jointly by theorists and experimentalists. And that was a very exciting time to be there because there was a great enthusiasm for applying quantum theory to make new materials for the telephone system. While working at Bell Labs, Bardeen developed the theory of semiconductors, which eventually led to the revolutionary invention of transistors. (For this work, he and two colleagues received the Nobel Prize in 1956.) Then Bardeen left for the University of Illinois, where he became fascinated by superconductivity, which promised to fulfill the medieval dream of the perpetuum mobile, the frictionless machine that in principle might go on working forever. In 1957 he contributed to a theory that became the benchmark in that domain, and for that he shared the 1972 Nobel Prize with two new colleagues. This is how he explains why he moved from Bell Labs: One reason I left to come to the University of Illinois in 1951 is that I thought that superconductivity was a just purely theoretical thing with no practical applications and it would be better to work on it in an academic environment. And Fred Seitz, who was the first student of Eugene Wigner's in Princeton, a good friend of mine for many years, had come from Carnegie Tech, now CarnegieMellon, with some of his coworkers to establish a group in solid-state physics at the UniversityofIllinoisAndI University of Illinois. And I thought, if I came here with the group that was already present, they'd have a very strong effort in solid-state physics here. And that was true. It would attract the outstanding graduate students from places like Cal Tech and MIT; if they wanted to study solid-state physics their professors would send them out here as the best place to go. In sciences and in the arts, in business and in politics, location matters almost as much as in buying real estate. The closer one is to the majorresearchlaboratories major research laboratories, journals, departments, institutes, and conference centers, the easier it is for a new voice to be heard and appreciated. At the same time, there is a downside to being near the centers of power. No one is more aware of this than Donald Campbell, whose warnings about the dangers young scholars run by being immersed too soon in a competitive, high-pressure environment are relevant beyond the confines of academia: I do think that environments make a difference. And the assistantprofessorshipsatBig assistant professorships at Big Ten universities in psychology, where you have to produce five papers a year for five years to make tenure, are far less ideal than the British system in which a Francis Crick need not publish for years and years, yet still be kept in the system on the basis of interpersonal esteem. So much less pressure and much greater freedom to explore and try out things without fear of failing. People are responding to these conditions adaptively, and they are getting out the five papers a yearforfiveyearsButtheir year for five years. But their freedom to be creative is being reduced by the pressure for quickness and number, and so is their ability to write a whole manuscript. Look, you have two job offers, both of them have reasonable teaching loads. In one job you are going to be under high publish-orperish pressure. In the other job you are going to feel adequate and under less pressure. Obviously the two universities have different national esteem levels. Which job would you take? I say clearly take theonewhereyouwillbefreeof the one where you will be free of tenure anxiety and be free to explore intellectually. As with so many other things we have learned from these people's lives, there is no recipe for deciding, once and for all, which place is most suitable for the development of creativity. Certainly moving to the center of information and action makes sense; occasionally, it may even be indispensable. In certain domains there is really only one place in the world where one can learn and practice. But there might be disadvantagestobeingwherethe disadvantages to being where the action, and therefore the pressure, is most intense. Where is the right place to be? Unfortunately, there is no single answer. Creativity is not determined by outside factors but by the person's hard resolution to do what must be done. Which place is best depends on the total configuration of a person's characteristics and those of the task he or she is involved in. Someone who is relatively more introverted may wish to perfect his act before stepping before the limelight. A more extroverted person may enjoy competitive pressures from the very beginningofhercareerIneither beginning of her career. In either case, however, choosing the wrong environment will probably hinder the unfolding of creativity. INSPIRING ENVIRONMENTS I wrote the first draft of this chapter in a small stone cell, seven feet square, with two French windows looking out over the eastern branch of Lake Como, in northern Italy, near the foothills of the Alps. The cell was inhabited by hermit monks about five hundred years ago, and it is built over a chapel dedicated to Our Lady of Monserrat. An earlier versionofthechapelslidintothe version of the chapel slid into the lake a long time ago. Now, from its windows, between the dense branches of laurel, oak, cedar, and beech trees, I can see, below the rocks on which the chapel is perched, the huge body of the lake rippling toward the south, like a fabulous dragon straining to break its chains. The walls of the cell are covered with graffiti left by earlier occupants of this secluded haven. They too had the good fortune of having been selected by the Rockefeller Foundation to spend a monthattheVillaSerbelloniinthe month at the Villa Serbelloni, in the hope that the grand views, the panoramic paths through the forests, and the romantic ruins would inspire in them fresh bursts of scholarship. "Hundreds of trails, / Thousands of pines, / Limitless are the views" goes a haikulike verse scratched by a Harvard visitor. "Generations of guests, / Ten thousand experiences, / Attainment of resonant harmony.""Sun on the waters" begins an entry from UCLA, "the waves aglitter, / birds in the branches, / the trees atwitter; / bells of Bellagio—a new day's birth. Scholars in the Chapel: Heavenonearth!"Anotherverse Heaven on earth!" Another verse, this time from Sussex University in England, ends: "...our graffiti, / Make grateful, / if grotesque entreaty, / That in this treeencircled chapel, / We taste the tree of learning's apple."*

There is ample precedent for such hopes. After all, the village of Bellagio, where the Villa Serbelloni stands, has been visited through the centuries by the likes of Pliny the Younger, Leonardo da Vinci, and the poets Giuseppe Parini and Ippolito Nievo—who once wrote from Sicily that he "wouldgladlyexchangeamonthin "would gladly exchange a month in Palermo for twenty-four hours in Bellagio"—all of whom sought to refresh their creativity in its magic atmosphere. "I feel that all the various features of Nature around me...provoked an emotional reaction in the depth of my soul, which I have tried to transcribe in music" wrote Franz Liszt during his stay here. And from the highest points of the villa one can see at least three other similar enclaves across the lake: the Villa Monastero, formerly a convent for nuns from good familieswhereItalianphysicists families, where Italian physicists now repair to meditate and discuss quarks and neutrinos; the Villa Collina, once the private retreat of German chancellor Konrad Adenauer, now a place for German politicians to congregate; and the Villa Vigoni, built by a patriotic count of the Napoleonic era, now used for conferences that bring together Italian and German scientists. The air of these mountains, the smell of the azaleas, the shimmering reflection of old church spires in the fjordlike branches of the lake, are supposedly conducive to the creationofbeautifulpaintings creation of beautiful paintings, gorgeous music, and deep thoughts. Nietzsche chose to write Thus Spake Zarathustra in the coolness of the nearby Engadine; Wagner loved to write his music in a villa in Ravello overlooking the hypnotic blue Tyrrhenian Sea; Petrarch was inspired to write his poetry in the Alps and in his villa near the Adriatic; the European physicists of the early part of this century seem to have had their most profound ideas while climbing mountains or looking at the stars from the peaks. The belief that the physical environmentdeeplyaffectsour environment deeply affects our thoughts and feelings is held in many cultures. The Chinese sages chose to write their poetry on dainty island pavilions or craggy gazebos. The Hindu Brahmins retreated to the forest to discover the reality hidden behind illusory appearances. Christian monks were so good at selecting the most beautiful natural spots that in many European countries it is a foregone conclusion that a hill or plain particularly worth seeing must have a convent or monastery built upon it. A similar pattern exists in the UnitedStatesTheInstitutefor United States. The Institute for Advanced Studies in the physical sciences at Princeton and its twin for the behavioral sciences in Palo Alto are situated in especially beautiful settings. Deer tiptoe through the immaculate grounds of the Educational Testing Services headquarters, and the research and development center of any corporation worth its salt will be situated among rolling meadows or within hearing range of thundering surf. The Aspen conferences unfold in the heady, thin air of the Rockies, and the Salk Institute sparkles over the cliffs of La Jolla like a Minoan temple;theideaisthatsucha temple; the idea is that such a setting will stimulate thought and refresh the mind, and thus bring forth novel and creative ideas. Unfortunately, there is no evidence—and probably there never will be—to prove that a delightful setting induces creativity. Certainly a great number of creative works of music, art, philosophy, and science were composed in unusually beautiful sites. But wouldn't the same works have issued forth even if their authors had been confined to a steamy urban alley or a sterile suburban spread? Onecannotanswerthatquestion One cannot answer that question without a controlled experiment, and given the fact that creative works are by definition unique, it is difficult to see how a controlled experiment could ever be performed. However, accounts by creative individuals strongly suggest that their thought processes are not indifferent to the physical environment. But the relationship is not one of simple causality. A great view does not act like a silver bullet, embedding a new idea in the mind. Rather, what seems to happen isthatwhenpersonswithprepared is that when persons with prepared minds find themselves in beautiful settings, they are more likely to find new connections among ideas, new perspectives on issues they are dealing with. But it is essential to have a "prepared mind." What this means is that unless one enters the situation with some deeply felt question and the symbolic skills necessary to answer it, nothing much is likely to happen. For instance, John Reed, of Citicorp, remembers two instances in his professional life, separated in time by several years, when he had beenespeciallycreativeBothof been especially creative. Both of these involved recognizing the main problem his company was facing and sketching out possible solutions. As with most creative moments, it was the formulation rather than the solution of the problem that mattered most. In both cases, Reed wrote letters to himself, more than thirty pages in length, detailing the issues his company was confronting, the dangers and the opportunities of the next years, and the steps that could be taken to make the most of them. The interesting thing is that both letters were written when Reed was farawayfromtheofficeostensibly far away from the office, ostensibly free to relax: the first on a beach in the Caribbean, the second on a park bench in Florence. He describes how the second "letter" came about: I write myself lots of letters. And I keep some of them. In September before the third quarter I had been kind of tired, working Saturdays and Sundays, and I had gone to Italy for a week, just to get away. I went first to Rome for a couple days, then I went up to Florence. I'd get up early in the morning, and I'd wanderaroundandIsatona wander around, and I sat on a park bench, sort of between seven in the morning and noon, then in the afternoon I'd go visit museums and whatever. And I had a notebook, an Italian notebook, and I wrote myself long essays on what was going on and what I was worried about. And it helped me get my mind organized. Then in the afternoons I wouldn't do anything. Then at the end of the third quarter I went through the organizational changes. Just recently I pulled out my original memo and it was amazing, the degree to which I had my mind arounditheoverlapmusthave around it, the overlap must have been 80 to 90 percent [between what he wrote in Florence and what eventually was implemented]. Both "letters" were spontaneous and unpremeditated, although the issues they dealt with had been fermenting in Reed's mind for many months. Then it took several more months, after his return to headquarters, to sort out the good ideas from the bad, partly through discussions with friends and colleagues. And then several more months had to pass before ways werefoundtoimplementthemBut were found to implement them. But without the "letter from the beach" and the "letter from the bench" it is doubtful that Reed could have found such a fresh perspective on the issues confronting his company. This example still raises the question of how much the beach and the bench actually mattered. Certainly the creative solutions to Citicorp's problems would never have come about if anyone else had been sitting on them. The question is, would Reed have come up with the problem and the solution if he had stayed in his Manhattan office? Whilethisquestionis While this question is unanswerable, the evidence does suggest that unusual and beautiful surroundings—stimulating, serene, majestic views imbued with natural and historical suggestions—may in fact help us see situations more holistically and from novel viewpoints. How one spends time in a beautiful natural setting seems to matter as well. Just sitting and watching is fine, but taking a leisurely walk seems to be even better. The Greek philosophers had settled on the peripatetic method— theypreferredtodiscussideas they preferred to discuss ideas while walking up and down in the courtyards of the academy. Freeman Dyson's education at Cambridge, England, owed much less to what he heard in the classroom or read in the library than to the informal and wide-ranging conversations he had with his tutor while strolling the paths around the college. And later, in Ithaca, New York, it was through similar walks that he absorbed the revolutionary ideas of the physicist Richard Feynman: "Again, I never went to a class that Feynman taught. I never had any official connection with him at all, in fact. But we went forwalksMostofthetimethatI for walks. Most of the time that I spent with him was actually walking, like the old style of philosophers who used to walk around under the cloisters." Will the new generation of physicists, crouched in front of their computer screens, have equally interesting ideas? When ordinary people are signaled with an electronic pager at random times of the day and asked to rate how creative they feel, they tend to report the highest levels of creativity when walking, driving, or swimming; in other words, when involvedinasemiautomatic involved in a semiautomatic activity that takes up a certain amount of attention, while leaving some of it free to make connections among ideas below the threshold of conscious intentionality. Devoting full attention to a problem is not the best recipe for having creative thoughts. When we think intentionally, thoughts are forced to follow a linear, logical—hence predictable —direction. But when attention is focused on the view during a walk, part of the brain is left free to pursue associations that normally arenotmadeThismentalactivity are not made. This mental activity takes place backstage, so to speak; we become aware of it only occasionally. Because these thoughts are not in the center of attention, they are left to develop on their own. There is no need to direct them, to criticize them prematurely, to make them do hard work. And of course it is just this freedom and playfulness that makes it possible for leisurely thinking to come up with original formulations and solutions. For as soon as we get a connection that feels right, it will jump into our awareness. The compelling combination may appearaswearelyinginbedhalf appear as we are lying in bed half asleep, or while shaving in the bathroom, or during a walk in the woods. At that moment the novel idea seems like a voice from heaven, the key to our problems. Later on, as we try to fit it into "reality," that original thought may turn out to have been trivial and naive. Much hard work of evaluation and elaboration is necessary before brilliant flashes of insight can be accepted and applied. But without them, creativity would not be what it is. So the reason Martha's Vineyard, theGrandTetonsortheBigSur the Grand Tetons, or the Big Sur may stimulate creativity is that they present such novel and complex sensory experiences—mainly visual ones, but also birdsong, water sounds, the taste and feel of the air —that one's attention is jolted out of its customary grooves and seduced to follow the novel and attractive patterns. However, the sensory menu does not require a full investment of attention; enough psychic energy is left free to pursue, subconsciously, the problematic content that requires a creative formulation. It is true that inspiration does not comeonlyinlocationssanctioned come only in locations sanctioned by the board of tourism. György Faludy wrote some of his best poems while facing daily death in various concentration camps, and Eva Zeisel collected a lifetime of ideas while imprisoned in the most notorious of Stalin's prisons, the dreaded Ljublianka. As Samuel Johnson said, nothing focuses the mind as sharply as the news that one will be executed in a few days. Life-threatening conditions, like the beauties of nature, push the mind to think about what is essential. Other things being equal, however, it would seem that a serene landscape isapreferablesourceof is a preferable source of inspiration. CREATING CREATIVE ENVIRONMENTS While novel and beautiful surroundings might catalyze the moment of insight, the other phases of the creative process—such as preparation and evaluation—seem to benefit more from familiar, comfortable settings, even if these are often no better than garrets. Johann Sebastian Bach did not travel far from his native Thuringia, and Beethoven composed most of hispiecesinratherdismalquarters his pieces in rather dismal quarters. Marcel Proust wrote his masterpiece in a dark cork-lined study. Albert Einstein needed only a kitchen table in his modest lodgings in Berne to set down the theory of relativity. Of course, we do not know whether Bach, Beethoven, Proust, and Einstein may not have been inspired at some time in their lives by a sublime sight and spent the rest of their lives elaborating on the inspiration thus obtained. Occasionally a single experience of awe provides the fuel for a lifetime of creative work. While a complex, stimulating environmentisusefulforproviding environment is useful for providing new insights, a more humdrum setting may be indicated for pursuing the bulk of the creative endeavor—the much longer periods of preparation that must precede the flash of insight, and the equally long periods of evaluation and elaboration that follow. Do surroundings matter during these stages of the creative process? Here it may be useful to make a distinction between the macroenvironment, the social, cultural, and institutional context in which a person lives, and the microenvironmenttheimmediate microenvironment, the immediate setting in which a person works. In terms of the broader context, it goes without saying that a certain amount of surplus wealth never hurts. The centers of creativity—Athens in its heyday; the Arab cities of the tenth century; Florence in the Renaissance; Venice in the fifteenth century; Paris, London, and Vienna in the nineteenth; New York in the twentieth—were affluent and cosmopolitan. They tended to be at the crossroads of cultures, where information from different traditions was exchanged and synthesized. They were also loci of social changeoftenrivenbyconflicts change, often riven by conflicts between ethnic, economic, or social groups. Not only states but also institutions can foster the development of creative ideas. The Bronx High School of Science and the Bell Research Laboratories have become legendary because of their ability to nurture important new ideas. Every university or think tank hopes to be the place that attracts future stars. Successful environments of this type provide freedom of action and stimulation of ideas, coupled with a respectful and nurturantattitudetowardpotential nurturant attitude toward potential geniuses, who have notoriously fragile egos and need lots of tender, loving care. Most of us cannot do a great deal about the macroenvironment. There is not that much we can do about the wealth of the society we live in, or even about the institutions in which we work. We can, however, gain control over the immediate environment and transform it so that it enhances personal creativity. On this score, there is much to learn from creative individuals, who generally take great pains to ensure thattheycanworkineasyand that they can work in easy and uninterrupted concentration. How this is done varies greatly depending on the person's temperament and style of work. The important thing, however, is to have a special space tailor-made to one's own needs, where one feels comfortable and in control. Kenneth Boulding preferred to think and work in a cabin overlooking the Colorado Rockies, and he also used to get into the hot tub intermittently to gather his thoughts. Jonas Salk liked to work in a studio where, in addition to the material he needed for writing on biology, there was a pianoandaneaselforpainting piano and an easel for painting. Hazel Henderson, who lives in a rather isolated community in north Florida to avoid the constant distractions of the urban centers, describes her daily routine: I like to run for about two miles every morning, and I have a special place to run to, which is a very beautiful spot, just about a mile from here, where there's a beautiful salt marsh, it's looking over the city. And if you look to the left, it's just absolutely wild and beautiful. And there are my favorite blue herons and curlews andthere'sfishjumpingandyou and there's fish jumping and you can feel this teeming, living activity. And then if I look this way, to the right, there's this beautiful little city with its little spires, it's very harmonious. And, you know, there is a kind of balance between the natural system and the human system. Robertson Davies crafts his intricate fiction in a house he built fifty miles north of Toronto, on a prehistoric seashore rich in fossils, "in a very nice position looking down, down the valley toward Toronto so that we can see the lights andlooktowarditandbegladthat and look toward it and be glad that we're not there." The sociologist Elise Boulding has worked out almost monastic routines to help the rhythm of her creative thinking: An early morning walk, and reflection. In that year, 1974, I spent a lot of time on my knees; I have a little prayer plot that's at the back of the hermitage. I am not sure I would do that now. In 1991 I am a different person than I was in '74. But, do a certain amount of reading, you know, like the saints and those who have been through spiritual journeys, and simply reflectionAlotofreflection reflection. A lot of reflection, meditation. I have spent time in Catholic monasteries, and I value very much the hours of office and so on. In '74 I followed the hours of office and sang them. Again, I am not sure I would do that now. But just lots of quiet, a lot of time spent just looking out of the window at the mountains, and meditating. In Finland many people know Pekka, an elderly Lapp whose official job is to supervise the social services in the northernmost part of the country. But Pekka also travelswidely:Hespendshis travels widely: He spends his vacations visiting Tibet to learn the beliefs and lifestyles of the monasteries, or Alaska, in search of the vanishing Inuit culture. When he is in Helsinki on government business, he is known for never sitting down until he feels that the office where the meeting is held feels right. If it does not, he will take the elevator down to the street, walk around until he finds some branches, or stones, or flowers he likes. He will bring these objects back to the office, place them here and there on the desk or file cabinets, and when he feels that the environmentlookssereneand environment looks serene and harmonious, he is ready to start business. Those who have to deal with Pekka generally feel that his impromptu interior decoration also helps them to have a better meeting and come to more satisfying decisions. Elisabeth Noelle-Neumann, an innovative and successful German scientist and businesswoman (a few years ago, in a list of the one hundred most influential women in Germany published by a business magazine, she was ranked number two), has mastered the art of personalizingherenvironmentHer personalizing her environment. Her office, in a remodeled fifteenthcentury farmhouse, is furnished with graceful antiques; her home on the shores of Lake Constance is filled with books and rare objects that reflect her personality. Because she spends so much time traveling from one place to another (about fifty thousand miles every year just by car), her Mercedes 500 is another important working space. While the chauffeur drives, Noelle-Neumann reads and writes surrounded by favorite audiotapes, bottles of mineral water, sheafs of notepaper, and bundles of ballpoint pens of variouscolorsWherevershegoes various colors. Wherever she goes, she takes a familiar microenvironment with her. To a certain extent everyone tries to accomplish something similar to what Elisabeth and Pekka do. We usually do it with our homes by filling them with objects that reflect and confirm our uniqueness. Such objects transform a house into a home. When we moved into a summer home in Montana, all it took to make the alien environment familiar was for my wife to place on the mantelpiece two colorful wooden ducks we had had for some timeWiththeduckssafelynesting time. With the ducks safely nesting along the wall, the empty space became immediately cozy and comfortable. We need a supportive symbolic ecology in the home so that we can feel safe, drop our defenses, and go on with the tasks of life. And to the extent that the symbols of the home represent essential traits and values of the self, they help us be more unique, more creative. A home devoid of personal touches, lacking objects that point to the past or direct toward the future, tends to be sterile. Homes rich in meaningful symbolsmakeiteasierfortheir symbols make it easier for their owners to know who they are and therefore what they should do. In one of my studies we interviewed two women, both in their eighties, who lived on different floors of the same highrise apartment house. When asked what objects were special to her in her apartment, the first woman looked vaguely around her living room, which could have passed for a showroom in a reasonably pricey furniture store, and said that she couldn't think of anything. She gave the same response in the other roomsnothingspecialnothing rooms—nothing special, nothing personal, nothing meaningful anywhere. The second woman's living room was full of pictures of friends and family, porcelain and silver inherited from aunts and uncles, books she loved or that she intended to read. The hallway was hung with framed drawings of her children and grandchildren. In the bathroom the shaving tools of her deceased husband were arranged like a tiny shrine. And the life of the two women mirrored their homes: the first followed an affectless routine, the second a varied, exciting schedule. Of course, furnishing one's house in a certain way does not miraculously make one's life more creative. The causal connections are, as usual, more complicated. The person who creates a more unique home environment is likely to be more original to begin with. Yet having a home that reinforces one's individuality cannot but help increase the chances that one will act out one's uniqueness. It used to be said that a man's home is his castle, in deference to the fact that at home one feels more secureandincontrolthananywhere secure and in control than anywhere else. But increasingly in our culture it could be said that a man's—and especially a woman's—car is the place where freedom, security, and control are most deeply experienced. Many people claim that their car is a "thinking machine," because only when driving do they feel relaxed enough to reflect on their problems and to place them in perspective. One person we interviewed said that about once a month, when worries become too pressing, he gets into his car after work and drives for half the night from Chicago to the MississippiHeparksandlooksat Mississippi. He parks and looks at the river for about half an hour, then drives back and reaches Chicago as the dawn lights up the lake. The long drive acts as therapy, helping him sort out emotional problems. Cars can be personalized by a variety of means: The make we buy, the color, the accessories, and the music system all contribute to an athome feeling in a vehicle that affords both privacy and mobility. In addition to cars, offices and gardens are spaces that can be arranged to provide environments that reflect a personal sense of how theuniverseoughttobeItisnot the universe ought to be. It is not that there is one perfect pattern by which to order our surroundings. What helps to preserve and develop individuality, and hence enhance creativity, is an environment that we have built to reflect ourselves, where it is easy to forget the outside world and concentrate completely on the task at hand. PATTERNING ACTIVITIES It is not only through personalizing the material environment that we are able to enhance creative thought. Another very important waytodosoisbyorderingthe way to do so is by ordering the patterns of action we engage in. Manfred Eigen, the Nobel Prize winner in chemistry, plays Mozart at the piano almost every day to take his mind off the linear track. So does the writer Madeleine L'Engle. Mark Strand walks his dog and works in the garden. Hazel Henderson, who struggles daily with the problems of the various environmental groups she helps organize, gardens and takes walks to refresh her thinking. Some ride bikes and some read novels; some cook and others swim. Again, there is no best way to structure our actions;howeveritisimportantnot actions; however, it is important not to let either chance or external routine automatically dictate what we will do. Elisabeth Noelle-Neumann rarely eats at the times other people usually eat but has her own strict schedule that fits her own needs. Richard Stern has a sort of rhythm. I've imposed on time a rhythm which has enabled me to function. Function as a writer, function as a father, a husband—not always the best one —as a university professor, colleaguefriend colleague, friend. He goes on to specify in more concrete terms what he means by "rhythm": My guess is that though it resembles other people's rhythms, that is, anybody who does work either has a routine or imposes on his life certain periods in which he can be alone or in which he collaborates. At any rate, he works out a sort of schedule for himself and this is not simply an external, exoskeletal phenomenon. It seems to me it has much to do withtherelationshipofyourown with the relationship of your own physiological, hormonal, organic self and its relationship to the world outside. Components can be as ordinary as reading the newspaper in the morning. I used to do that years ago, and I stopped for years and years, which altered the rhythm of my day. One drinks a glass of wine in the evenings at certain times, when the blood sugar's low, and one looks forward to it. And then of course those hours in which one works. Most creative individuals find out early what their best rhythms are for sleepingeatingandworkingand sleeping, eating, and working, and abide by them even when it is tempting to do otherwise. They wear clothes that are comfortable, they interact only with people they find congenial, they do only things they think are important. Of course, such idiosyncrasies are not endearing to those they have to deal with, and it is not surprising that creative people are generally considered strange and difficult to get along with. But personalizing patterns of action helps to free the mind from the expectations that make demands on attention and allows intense concentration on mattersthatcount matters that count. A similar control extends to the structuring of time. Some creative people have extremely tight schedules and can tell you in advance what they will be doing between three and four in the afternoon on a Thursday two months from today. Others are much more relaxed and in fact pride themselves on not even knowing what they will be doing later on today. Again, what matters is not whether one keeps to a strict or to a flexible schedule; what counts is to be master of one's own time. Longer stretches of time show the same variable structure. Freeman Dyson and Barry Commoner believe that one should make a major career change every ten years or so to avoid becoming stale. Others seem perfectly satisfied delving deeper and deeper into a narrow corner of their domain throughout their lives. But what none of the persons we interviewed ever said was that he or she did this or that because it was the socially expected thing to do at that particular time. So it seems that surroundings can influencecreativityindifferent influence creativity in different ways, in part depending on the stage of the process in which a person is involved. During preparation, when one is gathering the elements out of which the problem is going to emerge, an ordered, familiar environment is indicated, where one can concentrate on interesting issues without the distractions of "real" life. For the scientist it is the laboratory, for the businessperson the office, for the artist the studio. At the next stage, when thoughts about the problem incubate below the level of awareness, a different environment may be more helpful. Thedistractionofnovelstimuliof The distraction of novel stimuli, of magnificent views, of alien cultures, allows the subconscious mental processes to make connections that are unlikely when the problem is pursued by the linear logic learned from experience. And after the unexpected connection results in an insight, the familiar environment is again more conducive for completing the process; evaluation and elaboration proceed more efficiently in the sober atmosphere where the logic of the domain prevails. However, at any point in time, whatmattersmostisthatweshape what matters most is that we shape the immediate surroundings, activities, and schedules so as to feel in harmony with the small segment of the universe where we happen to be located. It is nice if this location is as fetching as a villa on Lake Como; it is a far greater challenge when fate throws you into a Siberian gulag. At either extreme, what counts is for consciousness to find ways to adapt its rhythms to what is outside and, to a certain extent, to transform what it encounters outside to its own rhythms. Being in tune with place and time, we experience the reality ofouruniqueexistenceandits of our unique existence and its relationship to the cosmos. And from this knowledge original thoughts and original actions follow with greater ease. The implications for everyday life are simple: Make sure that where you work and live reflects your needs and your tastes. There should be room for immersion in concentrated activity and for stimulating novelty. The objects around you should help you become what you intend to be. Think about how you use time and consider whether your schedule reflects the rhythmsthatworkbestforyouIfin rhythms that work best for you. If in doubt, experiment until you discover the best timing for work and rest, for thought and action, for being alone and for being with people. Creating a harmonious, meaningful environment in space and time helps you to become personally creative. It may help you achieve a life that reflects your individuality, a life that is rarely boring and rarely out of control; a life that makes others realize the possibilities for uniqueness and growth inherent in the human conditionButcreatingsuchalife condition. But creating such a life does not guarantee that you will be recognized as a genius, as a historically significant creative figure. To achieve historical creativity many other conditions must be met. For instance, you must be lucky, for to excel in some domains you might need the right genes, you might have to be born in the right family, at the right historical moment. Without access to the domain, potential is fruitless: How many Congolese would make great skiers? Are there really no Papuans who could contribute to nuclear physics? And finally, withoutthesupportofafieldeven without the support of a field, even the most promising talent will not be recognized. But if creativity with a capital C is largely beyond our control, living a creative personal life is not. And in terms of ultimate fulfillment, the latter may be the most important accomplishment.

6

Early Years

There is a certain amount of voyeurism involved in reading— and writing—about eminently creative people. It is a little like watching celebrity shows like Lifestyles of the Rich and Famous, where one is allowed to peek behind the facade into the living rooms and bedrooms of people whomweenvyfromafarButthere whom we envy from afar. But there is also a perfectly legitimate reason for reflecting on what happens to exceptional individuals from early childhood to old age. Their lives suggest possibilities for being that are in many ways richer and more exciting than most of us experience. By reading about them, it is possible to envision ways of breaking out from the routine, from the constraints of genetic and social conditioning, to a fuller existence. It is true that the accomplishments of these creative persons are to a great extent influenced by sheer luck—the good fortune of having been born withexceptionalgenesorofhaving with exceptional genes, or of having had a supportive environment, or happening to be at the right place at the right time. But many people with similar luck aren't creative. So beyond these external factors where luck holds sway, what allows certain individuals to make memorable contributions to the culture is a personal resolution to shape their lives to suit their own goals instead of letting external forces rule their destiny. Indeed, it could be said that the most obvious achievement of these people is that they created their own lives. And how they achieved this is something worthknowingbecauseitcanbe worth knowing, because it can be applied to all our lives, whether or not we are going to make a creative contribution. Hence what follows is not intended as light entertainment but as an exploration of how human potential can be expanded. CHILDHOOD AND YOUTH In our culture—perhaps in all cultures—some of the most cherished stories relate the childhoods of heroes. If a man or woman is held in high esteem, the popular imagination wants to find a sign of greatness as soon as possibleinthatperson'slifeto possible in that person's life, to justify and explain the success that followed. Here is one such story. As the fog slowly lifts, one after the other the bare hilltops burst from the shadows and blaze in the sunlight. A shepherd boy reaches into the pocket of his cape for an old crust and chews on it uneasily. His dog has been looking for some time toward the valley where the old mill stands, as if something is afoot down in the darkness. And now the ewes begin to stir. A yearling, scared by the tension in theairstartstobleatasiflost the air, starts to bleat as if lost. Then the shepherd boy hears the dry clip-clop of hooves coming up the rocky path and almost immediately sees the outline of a rider emerge from the shadows below. Who could this stranger be? He has only a slender sword at his side, so he is not a warrior; he wears none of the sacred symbols of the clergy; he seems to lack the caution of a traveling merchant. Yet he is certainly no peasant, richly dressed as he is in blue velvet hose and a golden mantle. What other sort of man can there bewhocanridesoeasilythrough be, who can ride so easily through the lonely hills of Tuscany in the Year of Our Lord 1271? The rider smiles down at the boy, shifting in the saddle. His eyes slowly circle the horizon. "Well, I think I am good and lost. I was trying to find the shortest road from Florence to Lucca, but after a full night's traveling, I seem to have left all human dwellings behind. Where are we, actually?" he asks, turning toward the boy. "And what name do they call you?" The shepherd gestures in the direction opposite to where the sun was rising. "If you followed the creek down there for two leagues, you'd be in the Valley of the Mugello. To the left is the road to Florence, and to the right the one to Lucca. And my name is Angiolo, son of Bondone." At this the rider nods, then yawns. He looks around at the ridges rising and falling like the waves of a tawny sea, and then, as if shaking himself awake from sleep, he slides of the saddle. "Sweet Mother of God, but I am tired. I hope, Angiolotto, that you have some fresh ewe's milk, because I haven't stopped to eat since this past noon. Don't worry, I will pay you well for it," he says, jingling coins in the fancy red leather purse that hangs from his belt. Angiolo uncovers a piece of cheese and the jar of milk he has kept behind a slab of granite. He apologizes to the rider for having no bread to of er, but the gentleman takes out afresh chestnutpiefromhissaddlebag chestnut pie from his saddlebag, which they share. After they have eaten in silence for a while, the boy cannot resist asking "May I query, my Lord, what takes you to Lucca? I would wager you are not from these parts." "And the wager would be yours. I was born up in Lombardy, on the banks of the river Po. My master is Teboldo of the Visconti who earlier this year was crowned pope as His Holiness Gregory, the tenth of that name. I rode out two moons ago *fromtheFlaminiangateofRome from the Flaminian gate of Rome* on a mission from him." Angiolo is not sure what all this meant, but being a curious boy, he keeps questioning further. "And what kind of a mission would that be?" The rider smiles. "His Holiness wants the best craftsmen to come to Rome and make the Eternal City as beautiful as it deserves to be. I am supposed to find master builders, sculptors, and painters, and convince them to enter the service of His Holiness." The boy thinks about this for a while. "How do you find out who the best craftsmen are?" "Oh, one asks questions, listens to stories. One looks at the work in churches, in palaces." Here a shade of smugness passes over the features of the rider. "But I have also my own special test. I ask any man who is supposed to be good to draw a perfect circle, a cubit across, freehand. If he is really good, he will draw something that looks quite round. But few do come close without a compass or a *stringheldatthecenter" string held at the center."* Angiolo rummages among the ashes of last night's fire and comes up with a stick of charcoal. "What?" he asks. "You mean like this?" And with one smooth movement, he draws a perfect circle on the slab of stone from which they were eating. The pope's envoy scratches his head. He looks at the boy, looks at the circle on the stone. He looks away at the hills, now almost melting in sunshine. "Not bad, not bad at all. How about drawing *naturalthings?Haveyouever natural things? Have you ever* drawn people, or, say, animals?" Now it is Angiolo's turn to smile. He glances at the fat ram, sunning itself at his feet, the leader of the flock, and with a few quick strokes he has sketched it so vividly that all it lacks is the Lord's breath for it to start bleating. The rider from Rome becomes very thoughtful. This is a version of the story of how the great painter Giotto was discovered, a story that all schoolchildren in Italy have heard *orreadatsometimeorother or read at some time or other,* probably many times through their lives. There are illustrations in schoolbooks and texts of Angiolotto drawing his circle on the stone with the startled envoy looking on, or of his drawing the sheep while the rider holds his head in amazement. The story goes on to tell how the envoy took the boy to the workshop of the famous Cimabue, there to learn the fine points of painting. Giotto—as the boy was soon called —began to paint one astonishing picture after another. His fame soon surpassed that of his master, and he became known as the greatest artist *inItalyperhapsinallof in Italy, perhaps in all of* Christendom. It is a story that most educated people in Europe know and cherish. Unfortunately, like many good stories, this one reflects more our psychological needs than reality. When I recently searched for material on Giotto's childhood at a leading university library, I found 102 volumes on the painter. None of them claimed to have any information about Giotto's childhood or, for that matter, *about the first thirty years of his life. A typical biography starts as follows: "Accordingtoolddocuments "According to old documents, Giotto was born in 1266, at Vespignano di Mugello or in Florence, but nothing is known about his youth, there are only legends. The only facts are those of his artistic beginnings in Assisi, but even these are unclear and difficult to establish" (italics added). All the volumes agree that Giotto's style was extraordinarily novel, that he resurrected the dead art of painting and prepared the way for the renaissance of the arts that was to come a century later. But the precocity of his genius is the stuff of mythandthelegendsthatsprangup myth, and the legends that sprang up around his life are an indication of how much we need events to be predictable, to make sense. If someone becomes outstanding, we want to believe that unmistakable signs of greatness were there early for all to see. Whether it is the Buddha, Jesus, Mozart, Edison, or Einstein, genius must have revealed itself in the earliest years of life. In fact, it is impossible to tell whether a child will be creative or not by basing one's judgment on his or her early talents. Some children do show signs of extraordinary precocityinsomedomainorother: precocity in some domain or other: Mozart was an accomplished pianist and composer at a very early age, Picasso drew quite nice pictures when he was a boy, and many great scientists skipped grades in school and astonished their elders with the nimbleness of their minds. But so did many other children whose early promise fizzled out without leaving any trace in the history books. Children can show tremendous talent, but they cannot be creative because creativity involves changing a way of doing things, or a wayofthinkingandthatinturn way of thinking, and that in turn requires having mastered the old ways of doing or thinking. No matter how precocious a child is, this he or she cannot do. Mozart in his teens might have been as accomplished as any musician alive, but he could not have changed the way people played music until his way of making music was taken seriously, and for this to happen he had to spend at least a decade mastering the domain of musical composition and then produce a number of convincing works. But if the real childhood accomplishments of creative individualsarenodifferentfrom individuals are no different from those of many others who never attain any distinction, the mind will do its best to weave appealing stories to compensate for reality's lack of imagination. We all know the mechanism that generates such stories, because we have used it to make our own lives, or those of our children, more interesting and more sensible. For example, little Jennifer has a poem published in the junior high literary magazine; soon her parents tell their friends about the clever things she used to say as a toddler, and how shelikedtolistentonursery she liked to listen to nursery rhymes, and how early she was able to recognize written words, and so on. If Jennifer then goes on to be a real writer, the stories of her childhood are likely to become ever more clearly focused on her precocity. Not because anyone is consciously trying to alter the truth, but because as one tells a tale over and over, the tendency is to highlight what in hindsight we feel are the important parts and to eliminate details that contradict the point of the story. Our sense of inner consistency demands it, and the audience will also appreciate thestorymoreWitheachtelling the story more. With each telling, Jennifer's childhood becomes more remarkable. Thus are myths born. Prodigious Curiosity Children cannot be creative, but all creative adults were once children. Thus it makes sense to ask what creative individuals were like when they were children, or what sorts of events shaped the early lives of those persons who later accomplished something creative. But when we look at what is known about the childhoods of eminent creative persons, it is difficult to findanyconsistentpattern find any consistent pattern. Some children who later astonished the world were quite remarkable right out of their cradles. But many of them showed no spark of unusual talent. Young Einstein was no prodigy. Winston Churchill's gifts as a statesman were not obvious until middle age. Tolstoy, Kafka, and Proust did not impress their elders as future geniuses. The same pattern holds for the interviews we conducted. Some of our respondents, like the physicist ManfredEigenorthecomposer Manfred Eigen, or the composer and musician Ravi Shankar, displayed unusual gifts in their respective domains before their teens. Others, such as the chemist Linus Pauling, or the novelist Robertson Davies, blossomed in their twenties. John Reed, CEO of Citicorp, made a decisive impact on the banking industry in his forties; Enrico Randone, president of the giant Assicurazioni Generali insurance conglomerate of Italy, left his mark on the company he led while in his late seventies. John Gardner discovered he had a gift for politics in his midfifties, when PresidentJohnsonaskedhimtobe President Johnson asked him to be the first secretary of Health, Education and Welfare, and Barry Commoner decided to break away from academic science and start his environmental movement at about the same age. In all these instances of late blooming, the earlier years provide at best only glimpses of extraordinary ability in the domain they eventually turned to. If being a prodigy is not a requirement for later creativity, a more than usually keen curiosity about one's surroundings appears to be. Practically every individual whohasmadeanovelcontribution who has made a novel contribution to a domain remembers feeling awe about the mysteries of life and has rich anecdotes to tell about efforts to solve them. A good example of the intense interest and curiosity attributed to creative persons is the following story told about Charles Darwin's youth. One day as he was walking* in the woods near his home he noticed a large beetle scurrying to hide under the bark of a tree. Young Charles collected beetles, and this was one he didn't have in his collection. So he ran to the tree, peeled off the bark, and grabbed the insect. But as he did so he saw that there were two more specimens hiding there. The bugs were so large that he couldn't hold more than one in each hand, so he popped the third in his mouth and ran all the way home with the three beetles, one of which was trying to escape down his throat. Vera Rubin looked out of her bedroom window and saw the starry skies for the first time when she was seven years old, after her family had moved to the edge of the city. The experience was overwhelming. From that moment on, she says, she could not imagine not spending her life studying the stars. The physicist Hans Bethe remembers that from age five on, the best times he had were when playing with numbers. When he was eight years old he was making long tables of the powers of two and of the other integers. It's not that he was especially brilliant at this, but he enjoyed doing it more than anything else. John Bardeen, the only person to be awarded two Nobel Prizes in physics, was good in school—he skipped from third to seventh grade—but did not get interested in math until he was ten. After that, however, math became his favorite pastime; whenever he could, he solved math problems. Linus Pauling, also a double Nobel Prize winner, fell in love with chemistry before he even entered school, while helping his father mix drugs in his pharmacy. The physicist John Wheeler remembers: "I must have been three or four years old in the bathtub and my mother bathing me, and I was asking her how far does the universe go... and the world go...and beyond that. Of course she got stuck as much as I have always been stuck since." Robertson Davies wrote continuously in school and won prizes for his essays. As a young child, Elisabeth Noelle-Neumann, doyenne of public opinion research in Europe, built imaginary communities: "My favorite toy when I was a child was not dolls but wooden pieces to build up a village—trees, houses, fences, animals, and very different houses, for example, a town hall. And I would spend two or three days at a time when I was ten, twelve years old thinking up stories about the lives of the people in the village." Jacob Rabinow, one of the most prolific inventors in terms of the number and variety of patents registered, became fascinated with his father's shoe-making machine as a small child in Siberia, and since then he has explored and tried to understand every machine he has encountered. The neuropsychologist Brenda Milner describes herself as follows: The thing that has driven me my whole life, and I have always maintained this, is curiosity. I am incredibly curious about things, little things I see around *me. My motherusedtothinkthatIwas mother used to think that I was just very inquisitive about other people's business. But it was not just people, it is things around me. I am a noticer. The sociologist David Riesman says: "If you ask what drives me, I would say it's curiosity." Yet none of these individuals—not Darwin, not Riesman—were prodigies or even gifted children as we now define them. But they had a tremendous interest, a burning curiosity, concerning at least one aspect of their environment. Whether sounds or numbers, people orstarsmachinesorinsectsthe or stars, machines or insects—the fascination was there, and generally it lasted all through the person's life. It is true that these memories of childhood may be even more open to retrospective distortion, to the kind of romancing that has led us to mistrust the accounts of prodigious early abilities, like the one about Giotto. Perhaps these stories are also largely post hoc fabrications. I am reasonably sure, however, that they are not. When people in the eighth or ninth decade of their life describe their first fascination, they dosowithaconcretenessthat do so with a concreteness that seems genuine. Sometimes the material evidence is also present: an old telescope built in childhood, a battered book that served as inspiration many years ago, a juvenile poem or sketch. So while these people may not have been precocious in their achievements, they seem to have become committed early to the exploration and discovery of some part of their world. But where does such intense interest come from? That, of course, is the really important question. Unfortunatelyheretooadefinite Unfortunately, here too a definite answer has to wait until we know a lot more about creativity than we do now. Perhaps the best general answer we can give at this point is that each child becomes interested in pursuing whatever activity gives him or her an edge in the competition for resources—the attention and admiration of significant adults being the most important resource involved. Whereas later in life creative individuals learn to love what they do for its own sake, at first this interest is often motivated by competitive advantage. A child who getsrecognizedforherabilityto gets recognized for her ability to jump and tumble is likely to become interested in gymnastics. A boy whose drawings get more favorable comments than those of his friends will become interested in art. It is not necessarily the sheer amount of talent that matters but the competitive advantage one has in a particular milieu. A girl with very modest musical gifts may become intensely interested in music if everyone else around her is even less musical. On the other hand, a boy who is very good with numbers is unlikely to get involved in mathematicsifhisbrotheris mathematics if his brother is already known as gifted in math, because as the younger sibling he would have to grow up in the older one's shadow. He may choose to develop his second best suit and become interested in something else instead. In some cases, the competitive edge is the result of the child's heredity—what's bred in the bone, so to speak. Especially among musically and mathematically gifted children, superior performance shows itself with such force that the audience has no choice but to recognizeit(providedofcourse recognize it (provided, of course, that the audience knows enough about music or math). In such cases, children will usually accept the gift of their ancestors and become more and more interested in developing it. In other cases—probably the majority—the initial curiosity is sparked by some feature of the social environment. Subrahmanyan Chandrasekhar, who won the Nobel Prize in physics in 1983, was the nephew of the first scientist in India to earn the same prize in 1930. As a boy, everyone in the family expected him to emulate the eminent uncle. Chandrasekhar knew that if hewantedtobeacceptedand he wanted to be accepted and admired by his relatives he had better become interested in science. However, not every creative scientist was interested in science as a child, nor was every creative writer committed to writing at an early age. A good example of the kind of career shifts that are common is the case of young Jonas Salk, who eventually discovered the polio vaccine named after him: Well, as a child, I wanted to study law, so as to be elected to Congress and make just laws. ThiswaswhenIwaseightyears This was when I was eight years old or thereabouts, ten years old. And then I decided to study medicine for reasons that had to do with my mother feeling that I wouldn't make a good lawyer because I could never win an argument with her. Hilde Domin, the eminent German poet, wrote her first poem when she reached middle age, after her mother's death; and she did not start publishing her poetry until even later. Jane Kramer, who became a pioneering TV producer and later dean of the Columbia School of Journalismwasnotawareofher Journalism, was not aware of her vocation until she was in her twenties. György Faludy switched to poetry only after he discovered that he could not draw. Another poet, Anthony Hecht, said: When I was very young, I felt that the greatest aptitude I had was for music, not poetry. And I think this was an inhibiting factor for me in trying to be a poet. I was thinking too much in musical terms, I was trying too hard to achieve musical effects, I was thinking and wishing that I could convert poetry into abstract musicAndoneofthethingsIhad music. And one of the things I had to learn was to stop thinking that way. It took enormous concentration and determination. But even though these individuals may not have known what specific form their curiosity would take, they were open to the world around them and interested in finding out about it, in living life as fully as possible. Few paths were as convoluted as that of the chemist Ilya*

Prigogine, who received the Nobel Prize in 1977. The son of a Russian emigré aristocratasayoungmanin aristocrat, as a young man in Belgium he was mainly interested in philosophy, art, and music. His family, however, insisted that he study a respectable profession, and so he enrolled in law at the university. As he read criminal law, he became interested in the psychology of the criminal mind. Dissatisfied with superficial knowledge, he decided to understand better the underlying brain mechanisms that might explain deviant behavior, and this led him to the study of neurochemistry. Enrolled in the chemistry department of the university, he realizedthathisinitialinterestwas realized that his initial interest was perhaps too amibitious, and started basic research in the chemistry of self-organizing systems. But Prigogine continued to be inspired by his initial curiosity; he gradually realized that the statistical unpredictability in the behavior of simple molecules might shed light on some of the basic problems of philosophy, such as the question of choice, of responsibility, of freedom. Whereas the physical laws of Newton and Einstein were deterministic and expressed certitudes that applied equally to thepastandtothefuturePrigogine the past and to the future, Prigogine found in the unstable chemical systems he studied processes that could not be predicted with certainty, and that could not be reversed once they happened. If you can say that the universe is deterministic, a kind of automaton, then how can we hold to the idea of responsibility? All of Western philosophy was dominated by this problem. It seemed to me that we had to choose between a scientific view which was negating humanistic tradition, or a humanistic tradition whichwastryingtodestroywhat which was trying to destroy what we learned from science...I was very sensitive to this conflict because I came to science, to hard science, from the human sciences.... But what I learned from thermodynamics confirmed my philosophical point of view. And gave me the energy to continue to look on a deeper interpretation of time and of the laws of nature. So, I would say, it is a kind of feedback between the humanistic and the scientific point of view. The synergy between the humanisticandthescientificquest humanistic and the scientific quest has served Prigogine well. In addition to illuminating basic thermodynamic processes, his ideas have inspired a great variety of scholars in the natural and the social sciences. Concepts he familiarized such as "dissipative structures" and "self-organizing systems," have found their way into discussions of urban planning and personality development. But like the molecular systems he studies, Prigogine's career could not have been predicted from a knowledge of his initial interests alone. It took the subtle interaction between his curiositythedesiresofhisparents curiosity, the desires of his parents, the opportunities offered by the intellectual environment in which he lived, and the results of his experiments to give shape to that conceptual system we now associate with his name. The Influence of Parents In most cases it is the parents who are responsible for stimulating and directing the child's interest. Sometimes the only contribution of the parents to their child's intellectual development is treating him or her like a fellow adult. DonaldCampbellwhosemany Donald Campbell, whose many novel methodological and theoretical contributions have enriched contemporary psychology, is one of the many respondents who feel "blessed" that his parents never talked down to them, and listened to their opinions about all sorts of adult issues. What the novelist Robertson Davies says is typical of many other respondents: My parents were like all parents. A hundred different things, it's very hard to describe what they all were. But one of the things they were, which I very, verygreatlyappreciate:They very greatly appreciate: They were very generous. They never denied their children anything that would help them. And they were very generous to me because I showed an aptitude for education, and so they helped me get a lot of education. And also they helped me to get a kind of grounding in music and literature by their example and their advice, and just by sending me where that was to be found. And so I have great cause to be grateful to them. And though often we had strong differences of opinion, I always feel that they were very kind and generoustome generous to me. In other cases the entire family is mobilized to help shape the child's interest. Elisabeth Noelle-Neumann and each of her sisters had an aunt or uncle deputized to take them to museums and concerts at least twice a month. It was important, she says, that each sister had her own exclusive area of expertise—the one who was always taken to the ballet was not taken to the art museum and vice versa. This way sibling rivalry was minimized and personal interest reinforced. A fairly typical childhood is the onerecalledbyIsabellaKarleone one recalled by Isabella Karle, one of the leading crystallographers in the world, a pioneer in new methods of electron diffraction analysis and X-ray analysis. Her parents were Polish immigrants with minimal formal education and limited means. Yet even during the worst years of the Great Depression Isabella's mother saved from her housekeeping money so that the family could take two-week vacations to explore the East Coast. The parents took their children to the library, to museums, and to concerts. Before starting first grade in the Detroit public schools, Karle hadbeentaughtbyherparentsto had been taught by her parents to read and write in Polish. "They were very good at introducing us to the world," says Isabella, "even though their resources were limited." She remembers being an excellent student, receiving her Ph.D. degree in chemistry fifteen years after entering the first grade. Her early interest centered on historical novels before she was introduced to chemistry. Yet she never took a science course until her junior year in high school, when a counselor advised that taking one would make it easier for her to get into a good college. So from a list ofcoursesinbiologychemistry of courses in biology, chemistry, and physics, she pointed at random to the one in the middle. "And the chemistry," she says, "fascinated me absolutely." So even though a child need not develop an early interest in a domain in order to become creative in it later, it does help a great deal to become exposed early to the wealth and variety of life. Strong parental influence is especially necessary for children who have to struggle hard against a poor or socially marginal background. Lacking other advantagessuchasgoodschools advantages, such as good schools and access to mentors, it is almost impossible to succeed without parental support and guidance. Oscar Peterson, the renowned jazz pianist, remembers that when he was a child his father, who was a porter on the Canadian railroads, used to set him the task of learning to play a piece of music every time he left on a trip from Montreal to Vancouver. As soon as he came back, his father made sure that Oscar had done his homework. If not, he would get "his bum kicked." But the most important influence of the family was building Oscar's senseofstrongpersonalstandards sense of strong personal standards and self-confidence, and encouraging his love for music: They didn't try to tether me and keep me in line. They would see me doing something and they'd say, "I think you know better than that. I think if you look in the mirror and take a good hard look you know you don't really mean that. That's not you." So they let me know that they had great expectations, more so than I was living up to at that moment. My family gave me, first of all, theloveofmusicTheyhelpedme the love of music. They helped me appreciate some of the music that I was hearing, and that of course catapulted me into the medium. But they also gave me a set of personal rules to live by that kept me from getting into some of the troubles that musicians were getting into at the time. And they gave me a certain amount of selfesteem by feeling that if I wanted to, I would do well. The sense of self-respect and discipline Oscar Peterson absorbed at home stood him in good stead later on, when the temptations of the jazzworldbecameacuteWhile jazz world became acute. While many of his peers succumbed to the easy enticements of sex, drugs, and liquor, respect for his parents and their values kept Peterson on a steady course: They let me know they would never tolerate or accept that [taking drugs]. I won't call any names, but a very famous musician once offered me cocaine —I guess it was cocaine—no, heroin, excuse me. As he called it, "a hit with heroin." And I told him quite frankly, "I would never be able to go home if I did this." Andthat'sthethingthatterrified And that's the thing that terrified me more than anything else. I couldn't figure out what I would tell my mother—far less my father —if I came home with a habit. There would be no reason for it. It wasn't a fear of what he would do to me, it was a fear of—maybe destroying him altogether. I didn't know how I could ever explain this to him. John Hope Franklin, the AfricanAmerican historian, remembers that his father, a lawyer, read all the time, so the son grew up thinking that reading was what adults did nightandday;andheremembershis night and day; and he remembers his mother as always supportive and encouraging. Franklin credits both parents for providing the intellectual and moral foundations of his life: I come from an educated parentage, you know. My mother was a schoolteacher and a graduate of the teachers' training program at Roger Williams University in Tennessee, and my father also attended that school. That is where they met. Then he went on to Morehouse College in Atlanta and graduated from there. ThenhestudiedlawHereadlaw Then he studied law. He read law in the office of a lawyer. That's what was frequently done around 1900. And he passed the bar with the second highest scores. He graduated from the University of Michigan and took the bar in the Indian Territory, not yet a state. Oklahoma was not yet a state. And so my parents had an enormous influence on my intellectual as well as my social development. I learned from them the value of studying and reading, that sort of thing. I learned from them too certain elements of honesty and integrity. I didn't havetowonderlaterwhetherI have to wonder later whether I should or should not do certain things. It was part of my being because of their influence. Manfred Eigen, the Nobel Prize— winning chemist, learned from his father the music he still plays and the high standards of performance his father expected. The historian William McNeill's father was also a historian, whose synthetic view of the past influenced his son's professional development. Freeman Dyson also remembers his parents fondly: Well, I was extremely lucky, of courseinhavingtheparentsthatI course, in having the parents that I had. They were both of them remarkable people. My father was this unusual combination of a composer and administrator, so that was a great inspiration to me, the feeling that you can do lots of things and do them all well. And my mother was equally unusual in a way because she was a lawyer and had read very widely and in fact was more of a companion to me than my father. They were both of them such strong characters. And yet still they left me complete freedom to do my stuff, which was science. And neither of them wasascientistbutthey was a scientist, but they understood what it was about. Parental influence is not always positive. Sometimes it is perceived as having been fraught with tension and ambivalence. Hazel Henderson modeled herself on her loving mother but resented the fact that she was so submissive to her patriarchal husband. Speaking of her father, she said: He would tend to be authoritarian because that's the way men were supposed to be. And so Mother never won an argumentIdidn'twanttobelike argument. I didn't want to be like him, although I realized that power was useful. And I did want to be like him in terms of, uh, well, I want to be effective, and I don't want to be trashed—I don't want to be a doormat. And so that was a tremendous tension in my childhood, what the hell to do with this. And so I think that, although I never verbalized it or thought about it at the time, I ended up deciding that I was really going to unite love and power. Often, especially in the case of artistsparentsarehorrifiedbythe artists, parents are horrified by the direction their child's interest is taking. Mark Strand, a U.S. poet laureate, started out with an interest in the arts. His parents "were not pleased when I announced my intention to be a painter. Because they were worried about how I would earn a living. And it was even worse when I expressed my intention to become a poet. They thought all poets starved, or were suicides or alcoholics." György Faludy had to take many university courses in various subjects to please his father, before turning to poetry. The generation of women representedinoursamplewere represented in our sample were discouraged by their families to consider science as a possible career. What chance did they have to become physicists or chemists? Better stick with the plan of trying to become high school teachers. As the above quotes suggest, parents were not simply a source of knowledge or intellectual discipline. Their role was not limited to introducing their children to career opportunities and facilitating access to the field. Perhaps the most important contribution was in shaping characterManyrespondents character. Many respondents mentioned how important a father or mother had been in teaching them certain values. Probably the most important of these was honesty. An astonishing number said that one of the main reasons they had became successful was because they were truthful or honest, and these were virtues they had acquired from a mother's or a father's example. Robertson Davies says this about his parents, both of whom were writers: They were very sincere about what they wrote, and I was broughtupIwouldnotsay brought up—I would not say strictly, because there was nothing harsh about it—but my parents brought me up in a kind of religious atmosphere so that I had a very profound respect for truth, and I was perpetually being reminded, because my parents were very great Bible-quoters, that God is not mocked. The German physicist Heinz Maier-Leibnitz, who trained two of his students to the Nobel Prize, believes that the responsibility of a scientific mentor is not only to be honest himself but also to make sure ofthehonestyofhiscoworkers: of the honesty of his coworkers: I don't know whether *the word honesty is the best word. It's the search for truth in your work. You must criticize yourself, you must consider everything that may contradict what you think, and you must never hide an error. And the whole atmosphere should be so that everybody is like that. And later, when you are head of a lab or an institute, you must make a great effort to help those who are honest, those who don't work only for their careers and try to diminish the work of others.* This isthemostimportanttaskthata *is the most important task that a professor has. It's absolutely fundamental.* Why is honesty considered so important? The reasons given share a common core, even though they vary depending on the respondent's domain of activity. The physical scientists said that unless they were truthful to their observations of empirical facts, they could not do science, let alone be creative. The social scientists stressed that unless their colleagues respected their truthfulness, the credibility of their ideas would be compromised. What theartistsandwritersmeantby the artists and writers meant by honesty was truthfulness to their own feelings and intuitions. And businesspersons, politicians, and social reformers saw the importance of honesty in their relationship with other people, with the institutions they led or belonged to. In none of these fields could you be ultimately successful if you were not truthful, if you distorted the evidence, either consciously or unconsciously, for your own advantage. Most of the respondents felt fortunate to have acquired this quality from the example of parents. Only in a few cases does parental influenceappearasathoroughly influence appear as a thoroughly negative force, an example of what the child wants to avoid in the future. Parents who are always quarreling, who are materialistic, who are unhappy with their lives, show their children ways not to be. But by and large it seems that parents are still the main source of the curiosity and involvement with life that is so characteristic of these creative individuals. This is true even when the parent is no longer alive. Missing Fathers A notable contradiction to the importanceofparentalhelpisthe importance of parental help is the fact that so many creative people lost their fathers early in life. This pattern is especially true for creative men. About three out of ten men and two out of ten women in our sample were orphaned before they reached their teens. George Klein, one of the founders of the new domain of tumor biology, is one of them. In a book of essays he describes at length the effect on his life of his father's death. He attributes both his sense of almost arrogant autonomy and the feeling of responsibility that drives him to thefactthathedidn'thavealiving the fact that he didn't have a living father to fear and to depend on. A young boy deprived of a father may feel a great sense of liberation, a freedom to be and do anything he wants to; at the same time, he may feel the tremendous burden of having* *to live up to the expectations he himself has attributed to the absent father. A fatherless boy has the opportunity to invent who he is. He will not have to stand in front of a powerful, critical father and justify himself. On the other hand, he will not have the opportunity to grow up andbecomeafriendandpeertohis and become a friend and peer to his father. The relationship remains frozen in time, and the psyche of the child always carries the demanding memory of the all-powerful parent. It is possible that the complex and often tortured personality of creative individuals is in part shaped by this ambivalence. George Klein ends his essay entitled "The Fatherless" with the following lines: Father, little brother, my son, my creator, you who will never allow me to know you, come, oppress me, crush me, mold me into whateveryouwantinto whatever you want—into someone I never was, never will be, if only I could tell you that... What would, I really want to tell you? Perhaps only this: It is wonderful to live—thank you for making that possible for me. I probably would have killed you if you had lived, but I was never truly able to live while you were dead. Although few mention their loss with such insight and pathos, in most cases the father's early death seems to leave a drastic mark on the son's psyche. Wayne Booth was raisedinaMormonfamilywhere raised in a Mormon family, where fathers are looked up to as God's representatives, almost godlike themselves. So when his father died, young Wayne felt a double blow: first the natural grief over losing his father and then the shock to his most basic beliefs: If Father was so powerful, how could he die? But again, with the grievous loss came an unusual gain: In the highly hierarchical Mormon family, at a very young age, he replaced his absent father, gaining the respect and high expectations vested in the oldest male. Wayne Booth's approach to his vocation reflects thisambivalenceofhisearlyyears this ambivalence of his early years. On the one hand, his approach to teaching, to literature, to criticism is informed by a deep respect for order and tradition; on the other hand, he has kept questioning accepted truths, maintaining into his seventies the open curiosity usually associated with youth. Sometimes the father, though alive, is virtually inaccessible to the son. Such was the case with the Indian composer and musician Ravi Shankar: I have to talk about my father a littleSeehewasaseekerInthe little. See, he was a seeker. In the sense that he was always seeking for knowledge. And he was such a learned person. In every subject. Starting from Sanskrit, to music. He was a lawyer by profession, he was in the Privy Council in London, he was with the League of Nations when it started in Geneva. He did his political science in French, almost nearing his fiftieth year. And toward five, six years from the end of his life, he gave up everything and started giving talks on Indian philosophy, even at Columbia*

University and foundationsinNewYorkHe foundations in New York. He earned a lot on different occasions, and he was offered fantastic jobs, you know, paying a lot of money, but he never saved. He didn't really look after us that way. My mother was separated from him at a very early stage. And he married an English lady, whom I haven't seen but I have heard about. So from my childhood on I saw my mother very unhappy and very lonely. But you know, she was such a great lady. She spent all her energy, time, and everything for the sake of us children. With very little moneythatwehadshereally money that we had, she really struggled to give education to my brothers. My father, as I said, was a very lonely person himself. And he lived away from his family, always. I have hardly seen him. If I add them up—two days, three days, maybe a week. [The] longest was once two weeks in Geneva we spent when he was with the League of Nations. I haven't seen him for more than maybe two or two and a half months altogether. So I had nothing to do with my father, unfortunatelythoughIrespected unfortunately, though I respected him and liked him very much. But I grew up very lonely myself, because I was the youngest. My mother was my best friend. The mere fact of not having a father is not what affects the later life of such children; what counts is the meaning they extract from the event. The death of a father is as likely to destroy a son's curiosity and ambition as it is to enhance it. What makes the difference is whether there is enough emotional and cognitive support for the bereaved child to interpret the loss asasignthathemusttakeonadult as a sign that he must take on adult responsibilities and try harder to live up to expectations. And here the mother becomes crucial, because in most cases it is to protect and comfort a loving mother that the child tries to work hard and succeed. The effects of a parent's death are often quite complicated. Brenda Milner's father, whom she adored, died of tuberculosis when she was eight. He had been a pianist and music critic for the Manchester Guardian. Because his job allowed him to spend many mornings at homehetookBrenda'seducation home, he took Brenda's education in hand and taught her the arithmetic tables and had her read Shakespeare to him. His death was "the worst emotional experience" in her life. After this event, Milner was drawn to science in part to avoid being overly influenced by her artistic mother, for whom she had a great affection when separated, but with whom she quarreled if they spent more than a quarter of an hour together in the same room. "I wanted to show that I was doing my own thing and not my mother's thing," she says of her decision to pursue science. "It was selfishperhapsbutitisvery selfish, perhaps, but it is very claustrophobic living with someone who has so much emotional investment in you when you are a child." In some cases, the support to the orphaned child may come from the larger community. When Linus Pauling's father died, the nine-yearold boy was taken on as the responsibility of the other pharmacists in Portland. Each day after school he would go to a different drugstore, and help his father's colleagues prepare medications, thus developing the initialinterestinthemysteriesof initial interest in the mysteries of chemistry that he had first acquired by helping in his father's store. Being orphaned certainly did not dampen Pauling's interest in the world around him: I don't think that I ever sat down and. asked myself, now what am I going to do in life? I just went ahead doing what I liked to do. When I was eleven years old, well, first I liked to read. And I read many books. My father is on record as having said, a few months before his death when I was just turning nine, that I was veryinterestedinreadingandhad very interested in reading and had already read the Bible and Darwin's Origin of Species. And he said I seemed to enjoy history. I can remember when I was twelve and had a course in ancient history in high school—first year—I enjoyed reading this textbook so that by the first few weeks of the year I had read through the whole textbook and was looking around for other material about the ancient world. When I was eleven, I began collecting insects and reading books in entomology. When I was twelve, I made an effort to collect mineralsIfoundsomeagates minerals. I found some agates— that was about all I could find and recognize in the Willamette Valley —but I read books on mineralogy and copied tables of properties, hardness and color and streak and other properties, of the minerals out of the books. And then when I was thirteen I became interested in chemistry. I was very excited when I realized that chemists could convert certain substances into other substances with quite different properties. And this was essentially the basis of chemistry. The difference in their properties interested me. Hydrogen and oxygengasesformingwaterOr oxygen gases forming water. Or sodium and chlorine forming sodium chloride. Quite different substances from the elements that combined to form the compounds. So ever since then, I have spent much of my time trying better to understand chemistry. And this means really to understand the world, the nature of the universe. While creative adults often overcome the blow of being orphaned, Jean-Paul Sartre's aphorism that the greatest gift a father can give his son is to die early is an exaggeration. There are justtoomanyexamplesofawarm just too many examples of a warm and stimulating family context to conclude that hardship or conflict is necessary to unleash the creative urge. In fact, creative individuals seem to have had either exceptionally supportive childhoods or very deprived and challenging ones. What appears to be missing is the vast middle ground. Another aspect of the family background that shows the same pattern is the social class of parents. Many creative individuals came from quite poor origins and manyfromprofessionalorupper many from professional or upperclass ones; very few hailed from the great middle class. About 30 percent of the parents were farmers, poor immigrants, or blue-collar workers. However, they didn't identify with their lower-class position and had high aspirations for their children's academic advancement. The psychologist Bernice Neugarten's father was a recent immigrant from Europe with little schooling who struggled to make ends meet during the depression. When she came home to Nebraska on a break from college, her father asked, "How do you like it?"Berniceexplainedthatshewas it?" Bernice explained that she was beginning to develop an inferiority complex because at the University of Chicago she was surrounded by so many Ph.D. students. "What is that?" her father asked. She answered, "If you just go to college and get a bachelor's degree, Dad, that is not as far as you can go. People can go on and take something you call a master's degree and something you call a doctor's degree." At which point her father waved a finger at her and said, "Then you should do that!" Only about 10 percent of the familiesweremiddleclassA families were middle-class. A majority of about 34 percent had fathers who held an intellectual occupation such as professor, writer, orchestra conductor, or research scientist. The remaining quarter were lawyers, physicians, or wealthy businessmen. These proportions are quite different from what one would expect from the frequency of such jobs in society as a whole. Clearly it helps to be born in a family where intellectual behavior is practiced, or in a family that values education as an avenue of mobility—but not in a family that is comfortably middle-class. The Mirror of Retrospection In looking back at childhood, it is inevitable that what we see is colored by what happened in the years in between, by present circumstances, and by future goals. A person who is relatively happy and content may remember more sunshine than there actually was, and someone wounded by life may project more misery into the past. We do know that adults who feel positively about themselves describe their childhoods in more favorable terms. What remains uncleariswhichisthecauseand unclear is which is the cause and which is the effect? Do these adults have a positive self-concept because they had happier childhoods, or do they remember their childhoods as happier because their adult self-concept is positive? In some of the interviews with fine artists that I conducted on and off for over twenty years, I noticed an intriguing pattern. An extremely successful young artist in 1963 described his childhood as perfectly normal, even idyllic. He went out of his way to assure me that none of the conflicts and tensionsonereadsaboutin tensions one reads about in biographies of artists had been present in his case. Ten years later, the same artist was having trouble professionally: His paintings were no longer fashionable, critics and collectors seemed to avoid him, his sales had plummeted. Now he began to mention events in his childhood that were definitely less rosy. His father had been aloof and punishing, his mother pushy and possessive. Instead of talking about the lovely summer days spent in the orchard, as he had ten years earlier, now he dwelt on the fact that he had often wet his bed and on the resultingconsternationthiscaused resulting consternation this caused his parents. Ten years later still, the artistic career of this no longer young man was pretty much washed up. His work was definitely in disfavor, and he had gone through two messy divorces, a severe drug habit, and was trying to control his alcoholism. Now his description of childhood included alcoholic fathers and uncles, physical abuse, and emotional tyranny. No wonder the child had failed as an adult. Which version of his early years was closer to the truth? Did the therapyheunderwentwhenthings therapy he underwent when things began to unravel help him see more clearly a past he had repressed? Or did the helpful therapist provide him with a script that explained and excused why he had failed? There is no way to choose among these alternatives with any assurance. It is possible that the early success had been a fluke, and the later failure was ordained by a miserable childhood. Or it may have been that the artist failed through no fault of his own, punished by the fickle changes in taste and market. In any case, there is a powerful pressure to make the past consistent with the presentYieldingtothispressure present. Yielding to this pressure provides a sense of subjective truth whether or not it conforms with objective events in the past. So it is possible that the reason our successful creative adults remember their childhoods as basically warm is that they are successful. In order to be consistent with the present, their memory privileges positive past events. Biographers convinced that the early childhood of creative individuals must include suffering may indeed find much evidence of grief that was not mentioned in our interviewsSimilarlyif interviews. Similarly, if biographers assume that a creative person must have had a happy childhood, they will presumably find quite a bit of evidence for that, too. The issue does not seem to be what were the objective facts involved. What matters more is what the children make of these facts, how they interpret them, what meaning and strength they extract from them—and how they make sense of their memories in terms of the events they encounter later in life. On to School It is quite strange how little effect school—even high school—seems to have had on the lives of creative people. Often one senses that, if anything, school threatened to extinguish the interest and curiosity that the child had discovered outside its walls. How much did schools contribute to the accomplishments of Einstein, or Picasso, or T. S. Eliot? The record is rather grim, especially considering how much effort, how many resources, and how many hopes go into our formal educational system. But if the school itself rarely gets mentioned as a source of inspiration, individual teachers often awaken, sustain, or direct a child's interest. The physicist Eugene Wigner credits László Rátz, a math teacher in the Lutheran high school in Budapest, with having refined and challenged his own interest in mathematics ("no one else could evoke a subject like Rátz"), as well as that of his schoolmates the mathematician John von Neumann, and physicists Leo Szilard and Edward Teller. Clearly, the teacher must have been doing somethingright something right. What made these teachers influential? Two main factors stand out. First, the teachers noticed the student, believed in his or her abilities, and cared. Second, the teacher showed care by giving the child extra work to do, greater challenges than the rest of the class received. Wigner describes Rátz as a friendly man who loaned his science books to interested students and gave them tutorials and special tests to challenge their superior abilities. Rosalyn Yalow, who earned a Nobel Prize in medicine althoughtrainedasaphysicist although trained as a physicist, remembers her interest in mathematics being awakened in tenth grade, when she was only twelve years old, by a teacher named Mr. Lippy. This is what she says about him, and the other teachers who had been influential: I was a good student, and they always gave me lots of extra work to do. I took geometry from Mr. Lippy. He soon brought me into his office. He'd give me math puzzles and math beyond what was formally given in the class, and the same thing happened in chemistry chemistry. John Bardeen became interested in math about the same age, influenced by a teacher who noticed his abilities, encouraged him, and suggested problems he could work on. As a result of this extra attention, when he took high school algebra at age ten he won the endof-the-year prize in a competitive math exam. The first teacher who took a close interest in the young Linus Pauling was a high school chemistry teacher by the name of William V. Greene: He gave me a second year of chemistrysothatIgotcreditfor chemistry so that I got credit for two years of high school chemistry. I was the only student in the second-year chemistry class. He asked me a number of times to stay for an hour at the end of classes and help him operate the bomb calorimeter. To keep up interest in a subject, a teenager has to enjoy working in it. If the teacher makes the task of learning excessively difficult, the student will feel too frustrated and anxious to really get into it and enjoy it for its own sake. If the teacher makes learning too easy, the studentwillgetboredandlose student will get bored and lose interest. The teacher has the difficult task of finding the right balance between the challenges he or she gives and the students'skills, so that enjoyment and the desire to learn more result. But given how famous the students in our sample became a few decades later, it is surprising how many of them have no memory of a special relationship with a teacher. This is especially true of those outside the sciences. Perhaps because a precocious math ability is easier to detect, teachers seem morewillingtoencouragefuture more willing to encourage future scientists than students gifted in the arts or the humanities. In fact, teachers are sometimes tarred uniformly with a black brush. George Klein found all but one of his teachers mediocre and felt that as a teenager he learned more about philosophy and literature from debates with some of his schoolmates than from any of his classes. Brenda Milner, the neuropsychologist, remembers how frustrated she was in school because she could not draw, sing, or do any of the things that were considered "creative" by her teachersBecauseshewasfiercely teachers. Because she was fiercely competitive, yet inept in the skills prized by her school, she turned into a workaholic in the subjects she was good at: I used to go home and undo the sewing that I had done so badly during the day, crying. I was also crying when I tried to draw a map of the Great Lakes and I could not get them to connect. There was nothing I liked to do better than algebra equations at night. I mean, it was just a pleasure. But I was not good at these handy-crafty things. And they liked to give prizesforartworkandallofthe prizes for artwork and all of the things I was bad at. You never got any recognition for Latin and algebra, and so on. Some of these exceptional students remember extracurricular activities more favorably than school subjects. Robertson Davies began to think of himself as a writer when he won most of the literary prizes offered by his school. John Bardeen knew he was good at math when he outperformed his older classmates in a prize competition. Elisabeth Noelle-Neumann could get away with much in school becauseshewrotepoemsthe because she wrote poems the teachers thought were beautiful. The future Nobel Prize physicists at the Lutheran school of Budapest were excited by the monthly competition that Rátz made up for his students. Every month a new set of problems was published in the intramural math journal, and the students discussed and debated them at length in their free time. Whoever solved the problems most elegantly by the end of the month won a great deal of recognition from his peers as well as from the teacher. The Awkward Years The teenage years are not an easy time for anyone. No matter how much care parents devote to their children during this phase of life, no matter how well suited the culture is to avoiding conflict between adults and adolescents, inevitable tensions emerge when children are between the ages of twelve and twenty. The necessity to adapt to physical changes, to regulate sexual urges, and to establish independence and autonomy while maintaining ties with family and peers are tasks that confront adolescents very suddenly and generallycausequitealotofmisery generally cause quite a lot of misery all around. Talented teenagers not only are not immune but have some special obstacles to surmount. For instance, they must devote time to the development of their interests and talents, which usually means that they are alone more often than other teens—practicing their music, writing their essays, or solving their math problems. They are on the whole less happy and cheerful as a result (though when alone they are significantly less miserable than their peers are). Youths with special talents also tend to be less sexually aware and less independent from their families than the norm. This is an important factor in their development, because it means that they spend relatively more time in the protected, playful stages of life in which experimentation and learning are easier to achieve. Sexually active adolescents meld quickly into the program of the genes, and if they achieve autonomy too early they become burdened by social responsibilities like getting a job, keeping house, and rearing children. Thustheyhavelessfreedomtotry Thus they have less freedom to try out the new ideas and behaviors that are essential to the development of creativity. At the same time, a youth who is not too interested in sex and depends on his parents is likely to be unpopular, a typical nerd. Another reason for the lack of popularity is that the intense curiosity and focused interest seem odd to their peers. Original ways of thinking and expression also make them somewhat suspect. Unfortunately, one cannot be exceptional and normal at the same timeParentsoftenfretandplotto time. Parents often fret and plot to make their talented children more popular without realizing the inherent contradiction. Popularity, or even the strong ties to friends so common in adolescence, tends to make a young person conform to the peer culture. If the peer group itself is intellectual, as in the case of George Klein and a few others, then the conformity supports the development of talent. But in most cases it is not. Then loneliness, however painful, helps protect the interests of the adolescent from being diluted by the typical concerns of that stage of life. None of the creative people we interviewed remembers being popular in adolescence. Some of them seem to have had a reasonably untroubled time, and others think back on those years with barely disguised horror; however, nostalgia for the teenage years is almost entirely absent. Marginality —the feeling of being on the outside, of being different, of observing with detachment the strange rituals of one's peers—was a common theme. Of course, a feeling of marginality is typical in adolescence, but in the case of creativepeopletherearreconcrete creative people there are concrete reasons for it. Some, like the sociologist David Riesman, recognize the necessity— in fact, the positive contribution— of this outsider role: "I had the advantage of my marginality— marginal to the upper class, marginal to my school friends, and so on, but also marginal because of my views, and at times, insulated." Others experienced long periods of illness, which required separation from school and peers. The physicist Heinz Maier-Leibnitz spent three months in bed and the restofoneschoolyearrecovering rest of one school year recovering from a lung ailment in the Swiss mountains. Brenda Milner and Donald Campbell complained of poor coordination in youth, which made playing sports or dancing rather difficult. These people did not persevere in their creative careers because they were more lonely than other children. However, when they found themselves on the outside, they were able to profit from it instead of lamenting their loneliness. Those who were somewhat precocious intellectually—such as JohnBardeenManfredEigen John Bardeen, Manfred Eigen, Enrico Randone, and Rosalyn Yalow—experienced another sort of marginality. They were promoted into higher grades and therefore grew up surrounded by older teenagers with whom they did not form close friendships. John Gardner remembers: "I moved very rapidly through school. This was a period when you were allowed to move as fast as you wanted to— provided you were able. So I finished the first eight grades in five years, and the result was I was with children older and bigger than myself." Performance in school matters more in some domains than in others. In mathematics and the sciences, the exposure one gets in high school is necessary for further advancement. Doing well in advanced courses is not sufficient, but it is a necessary condition for being accepted to a good college and then to a good graduate department, which in turn is a necessary step to a later career. But performance in high school is a poor indicator of future creativity in the arts and the humanities. Young artists, especially visual artistsarenotoriouslyuninterested artists, are notoriously uninterested in academic subjects, and their scholastic records usually reflect this. It is probably for this reason that the French—who reckon mental ability in rather rigid rational terms —say bête comme un artiste (dumb as an artist) when they want to put down someone's intellect. Certainly Eva Zeisel, an accomplished artist whose ceramic creations are exhibited in many museums, including the Museum of Modern Art in New York, felt that she was "not considered the bright child in the family" (it is true that she was being compared to uncles Michael andKarlPolanyiandcousinLeo and Karl Polanyi and cousin Leo Szilard). She tells how when she was seventeen she overheard a couple talking about her a few rows back at a concert: "Her grandmother is such a clever, bright, intellectual person. Her mother is such a beauty. And now look at her..." Michael Snow, the versatile Canadian artist-musicianfilmmaker, admits that he wasn't a very good student in high school and was surprised to be awarded the art prize in his senior year.

Ravi Shankar started touring with a musicaltroupeatagetenandafter musical troupe at age ten, and after that his education was conducted by his guru, an elder musician. THREADS OF CONTINUITY In some cases, the continuity of interest from childhood to later life is direct; in others it is strangely convoluted. Linus Pauling's interest in the material composition of the universe started when he worked in his father's drugstore. Elisabeth Noelle-Neumann's interest in her countrymen's opinions and values can be traced to her games with the imaginary inhabitants of the toy villagesshebuiltFrankOffner villages she built. Frank Offner remembers an important early event in his life: I know that I always wanted to play and make things like mechanical sets.... When I was six or seven years old, we were in New York and I remember at the Museum of Natural History there was a seismograph which had a stylus working across the smoked drum, and there were a couple of heavy weights, and I asked my father how it worked and he said, "I don't know." And that was the first time...you know, likeallkidsdoIthoughtmy like all kids do, I thought my father knew everything. But so I was interested in how that worked, and I figured it out. What makes this memory so interesting is that all through his life, some of Offner's most important inventions involved a stylus moving across a drum. For instance, he invented a crystaloperated pen recorder, "which made the cardiograph a hundred times better than anything anyone had done before," and he perfected the first EEG machines. Yet Offner saw nothing especially meaningful inthiscontinuityandwhenitwas in this continuity, and when it was pointed out to him, he shrugged it off. There are also cases in which the individual's adult theme harks back to the interests of an earlier generation. C. Vann Woodward, who revolutionized the way we understand the history of the American South, traces his interest in his vocation far back: That interest was born out of a personal experience of growing up there and feeling very strongly about it, one way or the other. I havealwaystoldmystudents:"If have always told my students: "If you are not really interested in this subject and do not feel strongly about it, don't go into it." And of course much of my writing was concerned with those controversies and struggles that were going on at the time, and what their background and their origins and their history were. The place I grew up was important. The environment and the time following the Civil War and Reconstruction. There was talk about that from my earliest recollections. It is the defeated whoreallytalkandthinkabouta who really talk and think about a war, not the victors. And I grew up in a family that came of slaveowning stock and were planters, and then in the small towns where we lived my father was a superintendent of the public schools. The artist Ellen Lanyon's maternal grandfather came to the United States from Yorkshire, England, to paint murals for the World's Columbian Exposition of 1893. Because she was his oldest grandchild, Ellen had the feeling that she was destined to inherit her grandfather'scallingandhis grandfather's calling and his creative spirit. And when I was about twelve years old, my grandfather died. My father and mother put together his equipment that was left plus new tubes of paint, et cetera, and it was presented to me on my twelfth birthday as a sort of, you know, a gesture. Passing the torch or something. And so I started painting, and I painted a selfportrait, the first thing I tried. I can absolutely remember the place, the room, you know, and everything. I don't know what happenedtothepaintingIt's happened to the painting. It's somewhere. I think that my mother has it. But in any case, I think that's the kind of beginning that sets a pattern for a person. Nowhere was intergenerational continuity more clearly evident than in the case of the physicist Heinz Maier-Leibnitz. He is a descendant of Gottfried Wilhem Leibniz (1646- 1716). At a distance of more than two and a half centuries, the parallels in their lives are quite astonishing. G. W. Leibniz is identified in the Encyclopædia Britannica as "philosopher, mathematicianpoliticaladvisor" mathematician, political advisor." Maier-Leibnitz is an experimental nuclear physicist and has been a scientific adviser to the German government. The elder one was one of the founders of the German Academy of Sciences in 1700; the younger was one of its recent presidents. G. W. Leibniz was elected a foreign member of the French Academy of Sciences because of his attempts to renew German and French intellectual cooperation after a war between the two countries; about 250 years later Maier-Leibnitz received the same honor for the same reasons. G. W. Leibnizdevelopedan"algebraof Leibniz developed an "algebra of thought" according to which all reasoning was supposed to be reducible to an ordered combination of basic elements. His descendant has been working on a procedure by which the truth value of television and newspaper stories could be evaluated by breaking them down into basic propositions. It should be added, however, that for each creative person whose life seems like a seamless unfolding from childhood into old age, or whose interests seem preordained even before birth, there is another whoselatercareerseemstobethe whose later career seems to be the product of chance or of an interest that appears seemingly out of nowhere long after the early years are past. WHAT SHAPES CREATIVE LIVES? We are used to thinking about the way a life unfolds in a deterministic fashion. Even before modern psychoanalysis, it was believed that adulthood is molded by the events experienced in infancy and childhood: "As the twig is bent, so the tree grows.""The child is father totheman"CertainlyafterFreudit to the man." Certainly after Freud it has become even more of a commonplace to assume that whatever ails us psychically is the result of some unresolved childhood complex. And by extension, we seek the causes of the present in the past. To a large extent, of course, such assumptions are true. But reflecting on the lives of these creative individuals highlights a different set of possibilities. If the future is indeed determined by the past, we should be able to see clearer patterns in these accounts. Yetwhatisastonishingisthegreat Yet what is astonishing is the great variety of paths that led to eminence. Some of our respondents were precocious—almost prodigious—and others had a normal childhood. Some had difficult early years, lost a parent, or experienced various forms of hardship; others had happy family lives. A few even had normal childhoods. Some encountered supportive teachers; others were ignored and had bad experiences with mentors. There were some who knew early in life what career they would pursue, while others changed their direction as they maturedRecognitioncameearlyto matured. Recognition came early to some and late to others. This kind of pattern—or rather, the lack of it—suggests an explanation of development that is different from the usual deterministic one. It seems that the men and women we studied were not shaped, once and for all, either by their genes or by the events of early life. Rather, as they moved along in time, being bombarded by external events, encountering good people and bad, good breaks and bad, they had to make do with whatever came to hand. Instead of beingshapedbyeventstheyshaped being shaped by events, they shaped events to suit their purposes. Presumably many children who started out with talents equal or superior to those of the ones we met in this group fell by the wayside either because they lacked resolve or because the conditions they encountered were too harsh. They never had an understanding teacher, a lucky break that led them to a scholarship, a mentor, a job that would keep them on track. So the Paulings and the Salks are the survivors, the gifted few who also were fortunate enough to make use oftheopportunitiesthatcametheir of the opportunities that came their way.

7
Creative Aging

There is still quite a bit of controversy among scholars about the relationship between age and creativity. When the topic was first studied, the findings suggested that creativity peaked in the third decade of life, and less than 10 percent of all great contributions were made by persons over sixty. Opinionsdifferhoweverabout Opinions differ, however, about what qualifies as a great contribution. When we look instead at total output, the picture changes. In the humanities the number of contributions appears to hold steady between thirty and seventy years of age; the trend is similar in the sciences, and only in the arts is there a sharp decline after sixty. In our sample productivity did not decline either; if anything, it increased in the later years. Linus Pauling at ninety-one claimed that he had published twice as many papers between the ages of seventy and ninety than in any preceding twentyyearperiod twenty-year period. Recent studies suggest that not only quantity but quality is retained with age, and some of the most memorable work in a person's career is done in the later years. Giuseppe Verdi wrote Falstaf when he was eighty, and that opera is in many ways one of his best— certainly very different in style fromanything ever written before. Benjamin Franklin invented the bifocal lens when he was seventyeight; Frank Lloyd Wright completed the Guggenheim Museum, one of his masterpieces, whenhewasninetyoneyearsof when he was ninety-one years of age; and Michelangelo was painting the striking frescoes in the Pauline chapel of the Vatican at eighty-nine. So although performance in many areas of life may peak in the twenties, the ability to change a symbolic domain and thus contribute to the culture may actually increase in the later years. WHAT CHANGES WITH AGE? One question in the interview asked about the major changes the person had experienced in the past two or three decades of life, especially withregardtohisorherworkThe with regard to his or her work. The answers are illustrative of how these creative individuals perceive the process of aging. In general, the respondents did not see much change between their fifties and seventies, or sixties and eighties. They felt that their ability to do work was unimpaired, their goals were substantially the same as they had always been, and the quality and quantity of their accomplishments differed little from what they had been in the past. Generalized complaints about health or physical well-being were almostentirelyabsentNotasingle almost entirely absent. Not a single person, even among those well above eighty, had anything but a positive attitude toward how they were doing physically, even though they were realistically aware of specific decrements and limitations. Surprisingly, when all the answers are taken into account, the number of positive changes reported is almost twice the number of negative ones. Part of this rosy picture is probably due to the tendency to put one's best foot forward in an interview situation. But given the general frankness of theresponsesIamleftwiththe the responses, I am left with the belief that we are dealing with something deeper than impression management. After all, it should not be surprising that if these people have carved out unique lives for themselves, they should also approach the end of life creatively. The answers to the question about what has changed in the last twenty to thirty years fall naturally into four basic categories. They deal with changes in physical and cognitive capacities, in habits and personal traits, in relationships with the field, or in relationships with domainsInadditionchangesin domains. In addition, changes in each of these four categories tend to have either a positive or a negative valence—thus generating eight possible kinds of outcome. Physical and Cognitive Capacities As we would expect, the most frequent changes mentioned had to do with the person's abilities to perform physically or mentally. About a third of the responses fell into this category. But we didn't expect that the number of negative changes reported would be balanced by an equal number of positiveonesHowcouldthisbe positive ones. How could this be true, given the generally dismal opinion we have of old age? Psychologists have long made a distinction between two broad types of mental abilities. The first is what they call fluid intelligence, or the ability to respond rapidly, to have quick reaction times, to compute fast and accurately. This ability is measured by tests asking a person to remember strings of numbers or letters, recognize patterns embedded in more complex figures, or draw inferences from logical or visual relationships. This typeofintelligenceissupposedly type of intelligence is supposedly innate and little affected by learning. Its various components peak early—on some tests it is teens who perform best, on some others it is twenty-or thirty-yearolds. Each later decade shows some decrease in these skills, and after age seventy the decline *is usually quite severe even among otherwise healthy individuals. The second type of mental ability is known as crystallized intelligence. It is more dependent on learning than on innate skills. It involves making sensible judgmentsrecognizingsimilarities judgments, recognizing similarities across different categories, using induction and logical reasoning. These abilities depend more on reflection than quick reaction, and they usually increase with time, at least until sixty years of age. In our sample of creative individuals, it is this kind of mental ability that is supposed to be improving, or at least staying stable, even in the ninth decade of life. When we look at what the interviews say, we find that the most common complaint is a decline in energy, or a slowing downinone'sactivityThisisa down in one's activity. This is a problem especially for performers: Ravi Shankar recalls nostalgically that even ten years ago he was like a tornado, cutting records in England, flying to India to do the soundtrack of a movie, jetting to California for a concert, all without missing a beat; whereas now, at seventy-four, he prefers to stay home, take his time, and focus on a few students and select performances. A few scientists also mention that they are getting slower and more cautious. Physicist Hans Bethe says thathemakesmoremistakesin that he makes more mistakes in calculations at eighty-eight years of age—although he is also more alert at catching mistakes than he used to be. Heinz Maier-Leibnitz, another physicist in his eighties, feels that while his appetite for doing things has increased, his energy no longer keeps up with his desire. Sociologist James Coleman recalls that twenty years ago he used to travel to a different city, check into a hotel incognito, and work four days and nights without interruptions with just a few hours thrown in for sleep—a regimen that he would not follow now. But an almost equal number of people said that in the last decades their mental abilities have remained the same, or have improved, a claim made most often by respondents in their sixties or seventies. This positive claim is based on the contention that because of greater experience and better understanding they can now accomplish things faster and better than before. For instance, Robert Galvin, who was seventy when he was interviewed, reports that his business decisions have become sharper and more effective because afterintensestudyhenow after intense study he now understands better the forces involved in international trade: We understood as we traveled around the world that there were some markets that were open and some that were not. Europe was fairly open, Japan was very closed. And we instinctively knew that that was not tolerable. We didn't know what to say about it, we couldn't write a fancy memo about it. We could only say things in an elementary way. So we went back to school, to learn from scholars. Scholars had this importantconceptcalledthe important concept* called the principle of sanctuary that was as applicable in business as in war. And all of a sudden what we instinctively knew became clearer to us. We now could think sharper and faster on issues of international trade. Barry Commoner feels that now he is much smarter and knows a lot more than he did a few decades ago. Isabella Karle believes that experience provides her with a knowledge that is more complex than it was earlier. Several agree with the poet Anthony Hecht that timehashonedtheirskillsAllof time has honed their skills. All of these positive developments are examples of crystallized intelligence, the ability to use information available in the culture for one's own ends. As far as it was possible to determine, men and women gave exactly the same 1:1 ratios of positive to negative cognitive outcomes. Habits and Personal Traits The second category of changes people reported involved issues of discipline and attitude. These were mentioned about a quarter of the timeandherepositiveoutcomes time, and here positive outcomes outnumbered the negative ones two to one. Negative changes almost always involved too much pressure and too little time, with the person taking the blame for not learning to avoid overcommitment. Other traitrelated problems included increasing impatience and guilt over not keeping physically fit. The positive outcomes featured diminished anxiety over performance, being less driven, and exhibiting more courage, confidence, and risk taking. Several respondents echoed Anthony Hecht'swords: Hecht's words: I probably am a little more trustful in unconscious instincts than I was before. I'm not as rigid as I was. And I can feel this in the quality and texture of the poems themselves. They are freer metrically, they're freer in general design. The earliest poems that I wrote were almost rigid in their eagerness not to make any errors. I'm less worried about that now. Several respondents mentioned having learned from past mistakes or criticism of their work. This kind oflearningcouldbequitepainful of learning could be quite painful. John Reed, the CEO of Citicorp, believes that after being "bloodied" in the market, when the stock of his company took a severe plunge that he blames himself for not having foreseen, his whole way of exerting leadership had to be modified: My approach to business has been much changed over the past ten years. I don't think I've lost any of my spark, or creativity, but I'm not quite as free. I don't have that absolute enthusiasm. It's been tempered by the realization that you can be wrong. I know some of myshortcomingsinspadesand my shortcomings, in spades, and I'm quite sensitive to them. And what I'm doing now, I'm doing quite well, but it's all discipline, it's not natural. In other words, I have disciplined myself to do these things and get them done, and I am working at it very hard. But it's not fun, and up till now, most things I have done have been fun. C. Vann Woodward has the historian's privilege of correcting *his own shortcomings more easily, by bringing out a new edition of his work: Well, I have learned more and I have changed my mind and the reasons and conclusions about what I have written. For example, that book on Jim Crow. I have done four editions of it and I am thinking about doing a fifth, and each time it changes. And they come largely from criticisms that I have received and those criticisms come largely from a younger generation. I think the worst mistake you could make as a historian is to be indifferent to or contemptuous of what's new. You learn that there is nothing permanentinhistoryItisalways permanent in history. It is always changing. So, as one who writes about it, I am one of those who change, but I hope not for the worse. The negative impact of time pressure was turned around by several respondents who felt good about having become masters of their own time. Again we see that the same event, in this case excessive demands on one's time and psychic energy, can have either a positive or a negative valence, depending on what the person does with it. But even when a person copes successfully with mushrooming demands, it is often impossible to master time completely. Elisabeth Noelle-Neumann describes how her methods of work have changed: They have become more orderly, more systematic. I developed many techniques during the last twenty years to cope with this terrible lack of time—it has become worse and worse. I thought it couldn't be, but still time got to be shorter. The astronomer Vera Rubin is verygraphicinherdescriptionof very graphic in her description of the demands on her time: The biggest challenge is to try to get enough time to do science. There are professional meetings, there are all kinds of organizations, there are committees. I am available at any hour of the day or night for any woman astronomer who has a problem, and that is certainly well known. So I may spend an hour a day involved in that kind of thing. It is just very hard to keep the time to do science, and I still really, really want to do it. And I am more privileged than most because I don't teach. But I think our expectations of what we can accomplish have gotten so high. I mean, there is the telephone and the fax and the computer. On bad days I have seventeen or twenty-four E-mail messages. Most days I really can barely handle my mail. I get lots of preprints and reprints and letters, and I don't have a secretary, which would help at some level. But if I read all the reprints and preprints and letters I could spend the whole day just dealingwithwhatcomesinthat dealing with what comes in that day. While men and women mentioned equal proportions of negative outcomes in terms of habits and traits, women reported more than twice as many positive outcomes as men did. Apparently creative women have an easier time adapting psychologically to the later years. Compared to men, they were especially likely to mention greater serenity and fewer internal pressures. Here again is Vera Rubin:*

Thirty years ago it was totally differentIwouldhavequestioned different. I would have questioned whether I would ever really be an astronomer. I mean, I had enormous doubts early on in my career. It was just nothing but one large doubt whether this would really work. It wasn't that I was able to persevere. I was unable to stop! I just couldn't give it up, it was just too important. It just never entered the realm of possibility. But I never was sure, really sure, that it was going to work and I would ever really be an astronomer. Relationships with the Field Another fourth of the responses dealt with changes in the relationship with colleagues, students, and institutions. Again, the number of positive and negative outcomes were about equal, but with one intriguing difference: All the negative outcomes were mentioned by men, whereas the positive ones were equally divided between the genders. Men apparently miss more the lack of formal institutional membership that age usually entails; they suffer more from retirement with its decrease in prestige and power. Eugene McCarthyleftttheUSSenatelong McCarthy left the U.S. Senate long ago; the sociologist David Riesman misses the scholarly conferences he no longer attends because he doesn't like to travel; the physicist Viktor Weisskopf like many of his colleagues in the sciences, is no longer involved in active research. But with age it is also possible to acquire a greater centrality in the field, or to develop new forms of association, especially with students. George Stigler spends more time on the prestigious journal he is editing; Ravi Shankar is planning the new center for the teachingoftraditionalmusicthatthe teaching of traditional music that the Indian government is about to build for him. The anthropologist Robert LeVine has decreased his trips to visit fieldwork sites in Africa, but he spends more time training thirdworld students. Manfred Eigen leads a giant laboratory in Göttingen, works closely with his twelve Ph.D. students, and is active in various scientific societies and government agencies. Relationships with Domains The last category of answers that respondents gave to the question of whathaschangedintheirlife what has changed in their life during the past decades has to do with the acquisition of knowledge. Contrary to the previous cases, where positive and negative outcomes were roughly in balance, the 17 percent of the responses that fell into this category were uniformly positive. It seems that the promise of more and different knowledge never lets us down. We can lose physical energy and cognitive skills, we can lose the power and prestige of social position, but symbolic domains remain always accessible and their rewards remain fresh till the end of life life. Some individuals discovered a broader set of possibilities within the domain they had been pursuing; one example is Nina Holton, who is fascinated with what she has been learning about sculpting in bronze. Some branched into new enterprises related to their past work: Freeman Dyson is now writing about science for the general public as enthusiastically as he used to do active science, and currently has a dual career as a mathematical physicist and a writer. Others discover an entirely new interest:HeinzMaierLeibnitz interest: Heinz Maier-Leibnitz writes cookbooks after having been president of the German Science Foundation. Still others simply look forward to being able to read more widely and to explore hitherto neglected realms of knowledge. Or they claim that in the past years they have learned to enjoy life more fully. Often the changes are not so much a matter of aging, or of the person deciding to change, but are dictated by the interaction with the medium, by the logic of the domain itself. The painter Ellen Lanyon describes theevolutionofherstyleinthepast the evolution of her style in the past decades: For a lot of my early work, I was labeled a sophisticated primitive because I was doing Chicago street scenes, but they were influenced by Sienese egg tempera painters of the fourteenth century. And consequently there was a certain kind of naive approach to perspective which was also premeditated. I was not naive. I was using a certain style. And in the late forties, that was quite appropriate. It was part of what was going on also in Americanimageryandespecially American imagery and especially regional imagery. Then because I moved through a period of time where I wanted to work on a larger scale, I worked with oil paint. And then in the very early sixties, by chance, I started to work from photographs. I worked from old family photographs. I worked from newspapers, sports photographs. I worked from old rotogravures that I found in Italy. And it was all figure painting. It was all nostalgia. You know, at that time to work from photographs was a taboo. I was actually working through the photographandtranslatingasort photograph and translating a sort of space or a pattern on the canvas that in its way resembled and was a view, a photographic view, of a particular situation that had occurred. It froze time. It stabilized a situation. Some of those photographs of the family were of deceased people. And a secondary reason was to take my own personal history, document it, establish it in time, so to speak, and therefore it was out and finished. I could set it aside, and I could go on. And that was a very important thing for me. And so therefore the work changed becauseimagerychangedand because imagery changed and moved. Next I went into the use of acrylics, which by that time were pretty well improved, and one could work with them. And I spent about five years training myself in the use of acrylics. So that now most people don't even know they're not oil paintings. In the process of doing that I resolved that I would also change the content. So I made another sort of cerebral decision, and I chose to work with the object, not the still life, but the object. And I wentthroughawholeseriesof went through a whole series of things, and it is at that point that the work became much more, I would say, metaphysical. The objects began to take on their own life. And it worked through a whole series that had to do with stage magic, early experiments with physics and chemistry. That started in about 1968, and the work is still involved in that general area. Then animals, birds, insects came in through the stage production. I mean, it all sort of proliferated and moved along. This quote illustrates well how inexhaustibledomainscanbeIn inexhaustible domains can be. In this case the different media of paint—egg tempera, oils, photographs, acrylics—different art-historical influences, changing emotional priorities, and maturing reflections on experience all interact and provide an endless series of developments that Lanyon can explore throughout her life. It is for this reason that changes in the domain are seen as being always positive; they allow a person to keep being creative even when the body fails and when societal opportunities become restricted. ALWAYS ONE PEAK MORE It is easy to see why these individuals see age in a more positive light than we may have expected. Every one of them is still deeply involved in tasks that are exciting and rewarding, even if they are ultimately unattainable. Like the climber who reaches the top of the mountain and, after looking around in wonder at the magnificent view, rejoices at the sight of an even taller neighboring peak, these people never run out of exciting goals. The actor Edward Asner expresses the sentiments of the whole group when he says that what absorbshisattentionnowis absorbs his attention now is demonstrating that my acting ability is better than it's ever been, doing it across the board, doing it however and whichever way I can. In as many ways as I can. Radio, commercials, voiceovers, narrations for documentaries, on-stage, TV, films. It doesn't matter. I thirst to...burst at the seams, eager for the chase. We asked respondents to tell us what their current challenges were, what goals absorbed their energies morethananythingelseAllthe more than anything else. All the answers were enthusiastic, describing in great detail the person's current involvement. It was clear that, like Asner, everyone was still "eager for the chase." The lone exception only confirmed this conclusion. Freeman Dyson, the one respondent who had nothing particular to work on at the moment, said that this was therefore a very creative period for him, because idleness was a necessary precursor of a productive burst: "I'm fooling around not doing anything, which probably means that this is a creative period, although of course youdon'tknowuntilafterwardsI you don't know until afterwards. I think that it is very important to be idle. So I am not ashamed of being idle." Some individuals, like the columnist Jack Anderson, let the challenge be determined by outside events; he was sure that interesting and important issues would keep coming up and present him with *opportunities for involvement: I always try to make the most important task the one that I am working on. I try to keep motivated by assigning a high prioritytowhateveritisthatIam priority to whatever it is that I am working on. I do not want to live in the past. I have had a few achievements in the past, but that is done and that is over with and I am glad that I did well. But that does not mean anything today. It is what I do today and what I do tomorrow that is important. This kind of future orientation was typical. There was very little reminiscing and dwelling on past success in this group; everyone's energies were focused on tasks still to be accomplished. The most frequent challenge was workingonabookandwritingof working on a book and writing of four or five articles during the next year. Some had outstanding research agendas to complete. A good example is the answer of Isabella Karle, whose esoteric technical jargon cannot entirely disguise the excitement bubbling under the surface of her quest: Well, right now, I'm studying a peptide system that makes channels in cell membranes, and it transports potassium ions from one side of the cell to the other. I am collaborating in this work with a man in India. He has been abletoisolateandpurifyIsay able to isolate and purify—I say this because many natural products come in many slightly different versions, and unless you can separate out these various different versions, you can't grow a crystal because it won't repeat properly, and a crystal has to have the molecules repeat in a certain fashion. He has prepared the materials and he has grown the crystals. In fact, the same material grows somewhat different crystals from different solvents. And I'm now looking at the third crystal form. Each one of them shows how a channel is formed. ThereisahelicalpeptideThe There is a helical peptide. The peptide has a big bend in it, and two peptides come together in an hourglass fashion like so. [She gestures.] They are hydrophobic on one side. That means that they are compatible with the kind of materials that make up cell walls. On the inside, they're hydrophilic, that is, they attract water or polar substances. So this channel in the crystal, in all the crystal forms, is filled with water, but it is interrupted in the middle by a hydrogen bond between two moieties, so that if you had a water molecule, it would not go throughthemiddleofitthrough through the middle of it, through the midportion. These materials are used as antibiotics, and that's how they perform their work. Well, it's very important in biochemistry, biophysics, to try to figure out how ions are transported because our bodies do that in all kinds of ways for all the foods that we eat, the minerals that we need. Another answer that suggests the multifaceted nature of these people's commitments is the schedule Rosalyn Yalow describes for her recent past, a schedule in whichscientificresearchpolicy which scientific research, policy making, family times, and public service are all intertwined: Well, let's see, on the 24th of February I lectured at Memorial Hospital here in New York City, and then at four and at six I met with women in science at Mount Sinai Hospital; then I went to the Eastern students' research meetings in Miami, and then I gave endocrine gland rounds the next day. Then I came home [to New York City] and I went to Auburn University where I lectured and interacted for three days;thenIwenttothePittsburgh days; then I went to the Pittsburgh conference, which is on spectroscopy, and then to an analytical chemistry meeting in New Orleans. I came back and then I went to the Stewart Country Day School and I spoke to their seventh to twelfth graders; then I went to Albany—all of this in the same week. Yesterday I spoke at New York Academy of Science to their high school gang. Next week I am going out to Lawrence Liver-more Laboratories in California. I am on the advisory committee for LawrenceLivermoreandLos Lawrence Livermore and Los Alamos. But I am giving a radiation lecture and I am speaking to the women's group. Then I go to see my daughter and her husband and my grandchild, and I come back on the 29th. On the 31st I leave to go to Nashville, where I am speaking at Vanderbilt for two days and then two days at the University of the South at Sewanee. Then I go back to California. The American Chemical Society is having a three-day symposium for which they borrowed my title "Radiation Society"Igetbackfromthere Society." I get back from there and then I am going out to Las Vegas for the American College of Nuclear Physicians, for some sort of meeting on radiation. For those like Barry Commoner, George Klein, Elisabeth NoelleNeumann, and Enrico Randone, who had been responsible for institutions—a business, a research lab—the main challenge is to continue helping the institutions survive. Here is what Robert Galvin says about his continued involvement with Motorola: Having given up the direct and operatingleadershipofour operating leadership of our corporation, I wish to remain fully active and influential in our institution. I am putting an incrementally greater amount of attention on those factors that I think will have leverage impact on the performance of the institution in the decades ahead, not just the weeks and months ahead. I think there are some significant fundamentals that show promise of allowing a commercial institution to elevate its performing capabilities. One of them that is on the Class A list for me is the vocational skill of creativitythepotentialfor creativity, the potential for changing the quality of leadership, which relates to the functions of anticipation and commitment. Some people have found unanticipated challenges thrust upon them, as it were. Jonas Salk was planning to devote himself to science policy and philanthropy when the AIDS epidemic intruded on the world. Salk found the challenge too* compelling to resist; he went back into the lab to try to find some immunological means to prevent the disease, just as he did with the polio vaccine many decadesearlierAdozenyearsafter decades earlier. A dozen years after retiring from a faculty position at the University of Chicago, Bernice Neugarten felt so distressed by reading statistics about the plight of poor children that she returned to doing policy research full-time. The dedication may be interpreted by some as workaholism, an obsessive inability to enjoy any other aspect of life except achievement. But this would be missing the point. For most of them work is not a way to avoid a full life, but rather is what makes a life full. The television producer Robert Trachingershowsthemultifaceted Trachinger shows the multifaceted nature of this process: I really want to enjoy life now. I've kicked back. I've always been a very hard worker, A-type personality. I used to have high blood pressure problems and take pills. Now I don't have to take pills anymore. I do some yoga, I do some tai chi. Teaching remains my great love because I get so much love and response from students, so much caring. That's important to me because the lonely ghetto kid is still very much a part of me. I have enough moneynowtolivecomfortably money now to live comfortably without working, or without teaching for that matter. I enjoy going to Europe and teaching young people in Europe, and consulting with the schools that I'm beginning to set up, departments of television and filmmaking. And I caution them about buying into our form of television because it's kind of cultural imperialism. Most of what they watch on television in Europe is American television, and it erodes their cultures. So we talk about these values. How do you develop responsible filmmakersandtelevisionmakers filmmakers and television makers who are not out simply to titillate audiences and make bucks? I'm going to school. I attend great books courses, and I'm fascinated by reading. If you came upstairs, I have easily fifteen hundred to two thousand books, many of which I've not read, but I hope as I get older I'll read, and I'll have more and more time to read. And I counsel young people. I am not a sage by any means, but I've lived sixty-seven years, and there are some things I do sense and do know. Caring is a good feelingandwe'velostour feeling, and we've lost our appetite for it. THE SOURCES OF MEANING According to Erik Erikson, the last psychological stage that people confront in their lives is what he called the task of achieving integrity. What he meant by this is that if we live long enough and if we resolve all the earlier tasks of adulthood—such as developing a viable identity, a close and satisfying intimacy, and if we succeed in passing on our genes and our values through generativity— thenthereisalastremainingtask then there is a last remaining task that is essential for our full development as a human being. This consists in bringing together into a meaningful story our past and present, and in reconciling ourselves with the approaching end of life. If in the later years we look back with puzzlement and regret, unable to accept the choices we have made and wishing for another chance, despair is the likely outcome. In Erikson's words: "A meaningful old age...serves the need for that integrated heritage which gives indispensable perspective on the life cycle. Strengthheretakestheformofthat Strength here takes the form of that detached yet active concern with life bounded with death, which we call wisdom..." The notion of integrity connotes the ability to tie together, to relate to others outside oneself. Erikson thought that the perspective of an older person is based on a new definition of identity, which could be summarized in the sentence "I am what survives me." If toward the end of life I conclude that nothing of myself is likely to survive, despair is likely to take over. But if I have identified with somemoreenduringentitiesmy some more enduring entities, my survival will provide a sense of connection, of continuity, that keeps despair at bay. If I love my grandchildren, or the work I have accomplished, or the causes I have championed, then I am bound to feel a part of the future even after personal death. Jonas Salk calls this attitude "being a good ancestor." In our study, we did not pursue directly the question whether and to what extent our respondents had achieved a sense of integrity about their lives. But answers to one question shed some light on the issueofwhatentitiesserveasthe issue of what entities serve as the kernel for the identity of this sample, the kernel around which a sense of integrity is likely to develop. The question was "Of the things you have done in life, of what are you most proud?" This question is certainly not ideal for studying integrity, because several respondents felt put off by the word proud and others were not too happy about singling out a particular accomplishment as the source of their greatest pride. Nevertheless, people by and large answered the question in a way that suggested they were thinking of the mostmeaningfulimportantthing most meaningful, important thing they had done in life and therefore of their main link to the future. Categorizing the answers was very simple, since all of them were basically of one type. As we would expect in a group of such successful people, what they had achieved in their professional life was the first kind of answer. About 70 percent of the accomplishments mentioned as sources of pride had to do with one's work. Surprisingly, however, 40 percent of the women and 25 percent of the men (a good 30 percent of the whole group) mentionedthefamilyfirstaswhat mentioned the family first as what they were most proud of. These are some of the reasons two men give for their answers: Well, I get a great deal of satisfaction and pride out of my children. And my grandchildren are absolutely delightful, because I *do not have to worry about when they misbehave. I turn them over to their mothers. Grandchildren are created, I suspect, for grandfathers to play with. My grandchildren are all beautiful and a great source of enjoyment. Now, my children, some of them havehadproblemsButbasically have had problems. But basically they have turned out pretty good. I have been very pleased with what they have accomplished and I am concerned about those who have problems. I am much more concerned about them than any of my problems. And I am more pleased with their accomplishments than I think I am pleased with my own. I get a good deal of pride from my family. Loyal, hard work in keeping the family at its best; my wife and children. The fact that my marriage has been stable—better thanstableit'sbeenreallyvery than stable, it's been really very fortunate—has been essential, I think, for my particular character. I think if I had not had a stable sense that that part of my life was OK, better than OK, if I'd had children that were failures, or if I'd had a divorce, I'm sure it would have affected the tone of what I write and also the teaching; I don't think I could have done the same kind of aggressive, bouncy teaching. As the second excerpt suggests, pride in family is often combined with pride in work. One could even concludethatalthoughthefamily conclude that although the family was mentioned first in this answer, its importance is subsidiary to that of writing and teaching. It sounds almost as if the family matters primarily because it enables the writer to concentrate all his energies on his task. In fact, family and work are usually so inextricably related that it is difficult to say from a single answer whether fame and accomplishments are valued because they enhance the family's well-being, or the other way around. It is striking, however, that no other themes intruded on this simple duality. In the last years of thetwentiethcenturyamong the twentieth century, among sophisticated people of supremely high achievement, one may have expected a greater variety and more esoteric topics on which to build a life's narrative. It certainly appears to vindicate Freud's deceptively simple answer to an inquiry about the secret for a happy life: "Love and work," he said, and with those two words he may have run out of all the options. In looking more closely at the answers, another interesting pattern appears. Some of the respondents— about 70 percent of the 70 percent whomentionedworkfirstassource who mentioned work first as source of pride—speak primarily about extrinsic reasons for feeling proud, such as the great contributions they have made, the recognition and prizes they received, their renown among colleagues. The remaining 30 percent emphasize intrinsic reasons—the cultural advance made possible by the accomplishment or the personal rewards of a difficult job well done. The physicist John Bardeen, although mentioning extrinsic reasons, emphasizes more the intrinsic importance of what he had beenworkingon: been working on: I think the theory of superconductivity. The two things I'm most noted for are being coinventor of the transistor and the theory of superconductivity. The transistors, of course, had much more worldwide impact than superconductivity, but superconductivity was more of a challenge. And the theory had much greater impact on other fields of physics. As for theoretical contribution, it opened up some new ways of thinking about the structure of the nucleus andparticlesofhighenergySoit and particles of high energy. So it contributed more to a deeper understanding of what the universe is all about, I think. The more extrinsic responses tended to dwell on the number of copies the person's books have sold, on the directorships of large research organizations he or she held, on the canvases displayed in important exhibitions—in other words, on the highlights of a job résumé. The economist George Stigler has a refreshingly direct answer to the question: I guess I have to say the things in whichIsucceededinimpressing which I succeeded in impressing other people with what I have done. And those would be things like the two areas of work in which I received the Nobel Prize, and things like that. So those and certain other work that my profession has liked would be the things, as far as my professional life goes, of which I'm most proud. Every other Nobel Prize winner, however, gave reasons that were intrinsic. Perhaps among these individuals who are so close to the top rungs of achievement in their fieldsonlythosewhohavereached fields, only those who have reached the highest stages can afford the luxury of playing down the importance of worldly success. But a closer look at the answers suggests that it is unwise to place too much weight on the answers to this single question. The reason becomes evident when we realize that almost 40 percent of the men gave responses that were coded as intrinsic, whereas none of the women did—every single one of them talked about the pride they felt in the extrinsic aspects of their contributions. Yet these women enjoy their workareinaweofitsimportance work, are in awe of its importance, and are much less interested in the fame and power it might bring them. It would be difficult to find a male scientist as much in love with his work as Vera Rubin, an artist as committed as Eva Zeisel, a historian as excited by his craft as Natalie Davis. So why did the women tend to emphasize external success in their answers to the question about pride? Probably because women have a much more difficult time gaining recognition than men, and therefore when they get it, it means more to them. In any case, this contradiction illustrates theimportantpointthattryingto the important point that trying to interpret a single answer out of the total context of what we know about a person can be deceptive. Isabella Karle, who at first gives a rather extrinsic response, in a different part of the interview, sounds definitely more interested in the intrinsic aspects of her work: I've been successful in the sense that I've had all sorts of scientific awards and have been elected to memberships in what are considered the "elite" societies. And I get invited to speak at all sorts of universities all over the worldandthat'sallverynice world, and that's all very nice. But I think that the biggest satisfaction is just doing, finding out something about nature that hasn't been known before. There's the satisfaction of seeing what some of these molecules look like. There's a satisfaction in seeing how they may react. I suppose it's very personal—why other people find satisfaction in playing a Beethoven sonata faultlessly, or painting a picture. Following the ins and outs of our respondents' answers to the question about pride, we conclude thatliketherestoftheworldthey that, like the rest of the world, they also stress in their personal narratives the twin themes of work and love. These are the sources from which they build a meaningful story about their pasts and a bridge to the future. The fact that they were lucky in having achieved a greater renown than most people get for their efforts does not seem to make much difference. There is no evidence that being awarded one or two Nobel Prizes gives a person a greater claim on wisdom or a surer defense against despair than having lived a full life as an honest plumber and parent. FACING THE INFINITE At the time of the interviews, all of our respondents were still actively involved in family and work projects that reflected the main themes of their lives. But often their interest had broadened to include larger issues: politics, human welfare, the environment, and occasionally transcendent concerns with the future of the universe. Interestingly, in entering the last decades of life, none of them appears to have embraced an orthodox religious faith. Fear of deathdidnotloomlarge;certainly death did not loom large; certainly not enough to send them to seek solace in a faith that had been alien at an earlier age. Those few who, like sociologist Elise Boulding, had strong religious foundations to start with continued in their beliefs. Yet even when a ritualized faith was missing, a broader faith seemed to be much in evidence: a faith in an ultimately meaningful universe, which imposes requirements of awe and respect—and curiosity—on men and women. Perhaps the closest anyone has come to a conversion experience is thepediatricianBenjaminSpock the pediatrician Benjamin Spock, who has been taken to task by religious fundamentalists and preachers such as Norman Vincent Peale for having introduced permissiveness into American child rearing and thus corrupted the national character. Now in his nineties, Spock is writing a book on spirituality. But his understanding of spirituality is a far cry from that of institutionalized religions: Spirituality, unfortunately, is not a stylish word. It's not a word that* gets used. That's because we're such an unspiritual country that wethinkofitassomewhatcorny we think of it as somewhat corny to talk about spirituality. "What is that?" people say. Spirituality, to me, means the nonmaterial things. I don't want to give the idea that it's something mystical; I want it to apply to ordinary people's ordinary lives: things like love, and helpfulness, and tolerance, and enjoyment of the arts or even creativity in the arts. I think that creativity in the arts is very special. It takes a high degree and a high type of spirituality to want to express things in terms of literature or poetry, plays, architecture, gardens, creating beautyanywayAndifyoucan't beauty any way. And if you can't create beauty, at least it's good to appreciate beauty and get some enjoyment and inspiration out of it. So it's just things that aren't totally materialistic. And that would include religion. All through her adventurous life the ceramist Eva Zeisel has tried to help the disadvantaged and has used her artistic gifts in part to advance left-wing causes that she sincerely believed would make the world a better place to live in. Now in her eighties, she looks at her past with objective eyes and, while not regrettinganythingisnolonger regretting anything, is no longer sure that her motives were the wisest. Although, without regrets or despair, she finds that the only thing she can absolutely rely on is the work she has produced, and perhaps the old goal of "doing good"—although she is less sanguine about that: I was thinking how to convey my accumulated wisdom to my granddaughter. And one of the things that I thought to tell her is that one tries to do good and one tries to produce something. I find that my craft helped me very much tomakelifemeaningfulbecause to make life meaningful, because once you make a pot and it is outside of you, it makes your life kind of justified and not flimsy. After all you go through, at the end you die, and it makes life much more...well, satisfying. It justifies your existence.... Then the question of doing good for society. Don't forget that all our contemporaries and ourselves had some big ideology to live for. Everybody thought he had to either fight in Spain or die for something else, and most of us had to be in prison for one reason oranotherAndthenattheendit or another. And then at the end it turns out that none of these great ideologies was worth your sacrificing anything for. Even doing personal good is very difficult to be absolutely sure about. It's very difficult to know exactly whether to live for an ideology or even to live for doing good. But there cannot be anything wrong in making a pot, I'll tell you. When making a pot you can't bring any evil into the world. For Mark Strand, the poet's responsibility to be a witness, a recorder of experience, is part of thebroaderresponsibilityweall the broader responsibility we all have for keeping the universe ordered through our consciousness: Yeah, I think that it grows out of a sense of mortality. I mean, *we're only here for a short while. And I think it's such a lucky accident, having been born, that we're almost obliged to pay attention. In some ways, this is getting far afield. I mean, we are —as far as we know—the only part of the universe that's selfconscious. We could even be the universe's form of consciousness. We might have come along so that theuniversecouldlookatitselfI the universe could look at itself. I don't know that, but we're made of the same stuff that stars are made of, or that floats around in space. But we're combined in such a way that we can describe what it's like to be alive, to be witnesses. Most of our experience is that of being a witness. We see and hear and smell other things. I think being alive is responding. The physicist John Wheeler is puzzling out something that sounds very similar to Strand's position, a quest after what has been called the anthropic principle, the idea that the worldexistsbecauseweexistan world exists because we exist, an idea that usually occupies theologians and philosophers. According to them, we know about the existence of the universe because we are conscious of it. Perhaps the universe is there only because we are conscious of it. But Wheeler, always a scientist, would like to formulate this vague and ambitious proposition so that it actually could be tested: Right now I am animated by an idea which may be totally wrong but I can't tell until I go further. That this great show that is going onaroundustheworldthat on around us, the world, that somehow we play a vital part in bringing it about. Thomas Mann expresses this somewhere in a vivid passage. And how can that idea be expressed in a way that is so clear that it is testable. Well, here I go, reading the works of the German philosopher Heidegger, and talk with everybody who has a prospect of being able to contribute to my point of view on this issue. It would be nice to bring it all to a particular focus on a particular issue that could be decided yes or no, but at this point the whole thing is so big, so unformedthatitisbetterto unformed, that it is better to nurture it. Jonas Salk, in addition to his immunological research, the concern for his institute, and membership on the board of philanthropic foundations, for many years considered the broader implications of evolutionary theory as it affects the evolution of culture and consciousness: I have continued to be interested in some larger questions, more fundamental questions, about creativity itself. This institution [theSalkInstituteforBiological [the Salk Institute for Biological Studies] was established with the idea in mind that there would be a crucible for creativity, a center for the study of creativity to explore with individuals who have exhibited that quality in the course of their lives. I see us human beings as a product of the process of evolution—I would say creative evolution. We have now become the process itself, or part of the process itself. And from that perspective, I have become interested in what I call universal evolution, the phenomenon of evolution in itself asmanifestinwhatIcall as manifest in what I call prebiological evolution, evolution of the physical, chemical world, then biological evolution, then what I call metabiological evolution, evolution of the mind by itself, the brain-mind. And now I'm beginning to write about teleological evolution, which is evolution with a purpose. So my purpose now is to try to understand evolution, creativity, in a purposeful way. Younger scientists often look at their elders with a certain discomfort. They scoff at the WheelerstheSpocksandthe Wheelers, the Spocks, and the Salks, implying that they might be going slightly soft in the head, because in old age they seem to throw all caution to the wind, break out of disciplinary boundaries, and start concerning themselves with the big problems of existence. While occasionally there might be grounds for dismissing these attempts as the vaporings of senility, the examples in our sample point in a different direction. Older scientists and artists who have spent decades within a narrow segment of their domain often feel a sense of liberation when, after they have left theirmarkonthedisciplinethey their mark on the discipline, they begin to explore the world outside the artistic studio or the scientific laboratory. As they do this, the problems they address are almost certainly going to be more intractable than the ones they faced earlier in life. Should they therefore desist, or be ridiculed? Or should we feel sorry instead for their critics, who judge human endeavor only by the strict and often sterile rules of a single discipline? Of course these questions are rhetorical, because as far as I am concerned the quest these men and womenareembarkingonisexactly women are embarking on is exactly what makes their stage of life so exciting and worthwhile. It is difficult to see how it could be otherwise. Wisdom and integrity cannot be found in any single domain. A broader viewpoint that breaks across disciplinary boundaries is needed, a way of understanding that combines knowing and sensing, feeling and judging. In facing this task one cannot expect to succeed in the public eye, as one can when a field of culture recognizes one's contributions to art, business, or science. But by this time a person aspiringtowisdomknowsthatthe aspiring to wisdom knows that the bottom line of a well-lived life is not so much success but the certainty we reach, in the most private fibers of our being, that our existence is linked in a meaningful way with the rest of the universe.*